THE IRISH (AND OTHER FOREIGNERS)

THE IRISH (AND OTHER FOREIGNERS)

From the first people to the Poles

SHANE HEGARTY ～

Gill & Macmillan

Gill & Macmillan Ltd
Hume Avenue, Park West, Dublin 12
with associated companies throughout the world
www.gillmacmillan.ie

978 07171 4451 8

Index compiled by Cover to Cover
Typography design by Make Communication
Print origination by Carole Lynch
Printed and bound in Great Britain by MPG Books Ltd,
Bodmin, Cornwall

This book is typeset in Linotype Minion and
Neue Helvetica.

The paper used in this book comes from the wood pulp
of managed forests. For every tree felled, at least one
tree is planted, thereby renewing natural resources.

A CIP catalogue record for this book is available
from the British Library.

5 4 3 2 1

CONTENTS

PREFACE

PREFACE

This book might be about the only useful thing that's come out of a late train. It was winter 2006, and I was shuffling about Dublin's Connolly Station desperately trying to kill time when I made the silent and utterly unoriginal observation that the concourse was clearly a mix of people from around the world. I followed that with the equally unoriginal thought that only a decade previously such a mix would have been enough to make a Dubliner drop his suitcase with surprise.

For most of its history, Ireland was known for its degree of homogeneity; for a palette that a paint manufacturer might have labelled 'pasty'. Foreign visitors were always notable; immigrants something to cause a little bafflement. Why would anyone come to Ireland? It was, and always had been, a place people *left*.

It was at this point I gave myself a mental jab and remembered that this was not actually true—that Ireland was for the span of its history a place to which mass migrations did occur. For a start, the first people had to have come from somewhere else, because they weren't some hardy bunch clinging onto the land as it was gradually cut off from the European land mass to its east. The whole Celtic idea, which the modern Irish base a large percentage of their identity upon, has for long been described as an invasion. I was in a city that had been founded by Vikings. And the line from Connolly Station brought people up North to a corner of the island still politically controlled by the government of the neighbouring island.

It was clear that Ireland's identity, although deeply affected by the experience of emigration, must have been shaped in part by its experience of immigration. And on a more personal level, I realised very quickly that I knew next to nothing about any of this. I knew vaguely about the first people; had only an immature understanding of the Viking invasions; and I was largely ignorant of how exactly the English had ended up here in the first place.

I quickly realised that when one starts to look at the history of migration to Ireland, one essentially begins to see that it forms something close to an alternative history of the island, from its pre-history to the present. This book, then, is the result of an attempt to build a potted history of each of these chapters in Irish history, plus a detour through some of the smaller migrations to have occurred in Ireland. It is not a political book. Nor is it an academic work. The aim, ultimately, is simply to give a broad sweep of this 10,000-year story. It is a layman's history of Ireland, and some of its more curious footnotes, through the prism of the occasional waves of people who came to the island—or in the case of the Celts, a people we thought came to the island but who may never have done so at all.

This is an outsider's approach to history, so has relied on the graft of a great many historians and archaeologists whose careers have been dedicated to unearthing the truths of Irish history, and whose work is often illuminating and deeply fascinating. These are people who have pushed forward our understanding of the past, and I am grateful to every one of those whose work informed this one.

I also wish to thank my employers, The Irish Times, for a sabbatical that was vital in getting this book written. I would particularly like to thank Hugh Linehan, Miriam Donohoe and Gerard Smyth for their understanding and generosity; and Joyce Hickey and Ruadhán Mac Cormaic for their wise and honest advice at a crucial stage.

Thank you to Michael Ryan of the Chester Beatty Library for his vital help. Any errors that remain are entirely my own.

At Gill & Macmillan, I wish to thank Fergal Tobin, Nicki Howard, Neil Ryan for their patience and enthusiasm for this project; Tess Tattersall for her keen eye during editing; and

Yann Kelly-Hoffman of Cover to Cover for not only compiling the index but also for a particularly important query.

And finally, I would like to thank my wife Maeve, who has suffered the stresses of this book with incredible fortitude, patience and understanding; who has endured endless conversations ending with anecdotes about Viking toilet paper or Brehon marriage laws.

Chapter 1 ∾

LATE TO THE PARTY:
THE FIRST IRISH

For a large monument, built on a hill, covering an acre and in good shape after 5,000 years, you would think that Newgrange would be easy enough to find. It is not.

You come off the motorway from Dublin, wind along the back-roads of Meath, leaning over the steering wheel in search of a sign. You know the giant tomb has to be there somewhere, but it's as if most of the signposts have been stolen and the rest swatted by a prankster.

It is thanks to one of these signs that the residents of St Mary's Villas in the nearby town of Donore became used to busloads of German tourists being dropped off in their housing estate. It's somewhat flattering to describe the mix of terraced and semi-detached houses as villas, but it is a pleasant area nonetheless. A few of the properties sport weathered For Sale signs. While St Mary's Villas has a few things going for it, even the most optimistic estate agent wouldn't consider it a wonder of the ancient world.

It's as if the authorities don't want you to find Newgrange. As it happens, they don't. They want you to instead find the interpretive centre on the opposite side of the River Boyne, from where you can take a bus to the monument for an organised tour. It's estimated that 8,000 car drivers discover this every year, when their GPS brings them, quite properly, to Newgrange, only for them to be sent back a few miles to wait for transport to take them there again.

If you want to go to the interpretive centre, then you have to know that you're following the directions for Brú na Bóinne ('Palace of the Boyne'). If, on the other hand, you are content to see only the monument's exterior, then it is best to follow the signposts for Newgrange Farm, with a tantalising footnote insisting: 'No access to the monument'.

At the farm you can pet lambs, feed horses and even sit on a tractor. But the real treat comes before you even get there. About a hundred metres from the farm's entrance, as the country lane narrows, you turn a corner and Newgrange suddenly sneaks into view; high, gleaming, far more mesmerising than pictures convey. You'll need to compose yourself in case you drive into a hedge.

In the late seventeenth century there was no interpretive centre, and appreciation of the monument was not always expressed in the most delicate of ways. Visiting in 1699, the Welsh naturalist Edward Lhuyd watched as the local landowner, Charles Campbell, instructed his servants to pinch its stone for road repairs. Campbell's men had been the first to discover the monument when digging through a bank in search of stones. They clambered into a passage knee-deep in stones and debris. The mound had slumped and its support slabs had fallen forward so that they were almost touching. Its importance, though, was almost immediately recognised, and some of the antiquarians who subsequently visited have left illustrations of how it appeared in the early years after it was unearthed. Which is lucky, because vandalism, carelessness, pilfering and the appetite for stone to surface the nearby road was not kind to it.

It would be more accurate to say that Newgrange was redis-covered in 1699 rather than discovered. The Romans had known all about it, had visited it and left a few valuables behind. The Vikings knew about it as well, and the various Irish kings of the region were fully aware of it.

It may have been better off staying forgotten in a Meath field for another couple of hundred years at least. The cremated remains of four or five people are known to have been placed there, but it's likely that there were actually several more and they've disappeared over the centuries, although quite when we can't be sure. We do know, though, that it was a bit of a gravel trove for local roads around the time it was found, and that the easy access meant that it was plundered, rearranged, damaged and scribbled on with some frequency before the twentieth century saw the imposition of restraint.

In the 1860s, John Murray's *Handbook for Travellers in Ireland* gave a clear idea of just how accessible the site was, informing tourists that, 'The passage is 63ft long, and is formed of enormous upright stones, 22 on one side and 21 on the other; and having forced himself through it with some trouble, the visitor emerges into a lofty dome roofed chamber.'

Those who followed these directions often left something behind. The ancient passageway has the names of many of those visitors carved into its stones.

In the eighteenth century, it was thought that the Vikings had built it for a dying warrior. Since then, we've learned a great deal more and by any measure, modern or ancient, the building of Newgrange was an astonishing achievement. A tomb, it is about 80 m in diameter and 12 m high. It was built around 3200 BC, which gives it a 400-year head start on the Pyramids. In all, 200,000 tonnes of rock went into building the monuments at Newgrange and the area around it. Boulders were brought from as far north as the Mourne Mountains and as far south as the Wicklow Mountains.

The construction of Newgrange couldn't have been a haphazard affair, but must have been meticulously planned. It involved perhaps six teams of workers, each with a specific task, and would have required astronomers, engineers, artists, drainage experts and labourers. Its roof was made using a succession of overlapping slabs, until the final one was 20 ft off the floor. It was then buried under a mound of earth and covered in the rolled quartz that

Campbell's men later used to surface nearby roads. It was topped off with a sophisticated drainage system designed to divert water away from the centre and keep the chamber dry. And it was all built without a metal tool. It is, in short, a marvel of the Stone Age or any age.

Archaeologists know a lot about Newgrange, but not everything. We can only guess at the meaning of the art etched into its stones. Several cremated corpses were originally placed in the chamber, but we've no idea how many in all, because by the time excavations began in earnest teeth and bone fragments had been scattered throughout it. Meanwhile, the strikingly neat vertical quartz wall that now hugs the front of the monument may never have been there in the first place.

Most of what we have since discovered about Newgrange comes from excavations carried out between 1962 and 1975, when a team led by archaeologist Michael O'Kelly unearthed its most famous feature: a roofbox at the rear of the chamber that was lit only once a year by the mid-winter solstice sunrise. This makes it the earliest astronomically aligned structure in the world. During the early morning of 21 December 1969, O'Kelly became the first person in modern times to have the privilege of standing in the chamber as it became flooded with sunlight. Today, a waiting list for the annual experience is years long, and even then there's no guarantee that the sun will co-operate in the spectacle.

When it does, it is humbling and magical and briefly links twenty-first century Irish with their prehistoric ancestors and beyond. It was built 4,000 years after the first people landed in Ireland, yet can be considered part of an almost continuous and evolving culture brought here by those original colonists. Newgrange still has its secrets, but it has reluctantly given answers to the many archaeologists who have spent their careers asking it questions. Not everything from that era has been so obliging. If you were looking for an area of archaeology that is so long on mystery but short on clues that it would make you snap your trowel in frustration, then Stone Age Ireland is as good a place as any to start.

———

We don't know much about the very first Irish. We're not entirely sure when they got here. We don't know exactly where they landed. We can only guess at where they came from. We don't know why they arrived or how many there were. What does seem increasingly certain is that humans came here long, long after they had colonised almost everywhere else in Europe.

The mass of rock that would eventually form the island of Ireland had been journeying slowly northward over several hundred million years, constantly submerging, resurfacing, experiencing changed climates as it moved across the equator. For much of the early aeons, Ireland was split in two until, 400 million years ago, those halves collided and joined along a suture that stretches north from the mouth of the Shannon. It means that fossil hunters find North American fossils in the west and European fossils to the east. If you wish to understand the ancient species of Kerry, the closest comparison is with the fossil record of eastern Canada.

Over these almost inconceivable stretches of time, great mountain ranges were forced up, then worn away again. Some 270 million years ago, a range known as the Hercynian stretched from southern Ireland all the way to the edges of Russia. The remnants of it are still there on the European continent, forming the mountain ranges north of the Alps, but if you trace them west they gradually diminish until they become the gentle hills and valleys of southern Ireland.

As for the animal species, we would know more about what lived here if ice sheets hadn't stretched down and rubbed away much of the rock that preserved the evidence. There is little proof of the large animals that must have roamed Ireland at various points over its long history. We get occasional hints, but little else. For example, in 1992, a Swiss undergraduate student, Iwan Stössel, was chipping away at rocks on Valentia Island, Co. Kerry when he noticed unusual indentations in the slate. It was a trail of 150 footprints left by an early amphibian that had dragged itself through a shallow tropical stream some 370 million years ago. This is the oldest set of footprints known to exist in the northern hemisphere.

The Irish rocks have handed up fossilised examples of spiders, dragonflies, armoured fish and various plants, but no dinosaurs. There are reptilian prints at Scrabo Hill, Co. Down that are from the Triassic period of about 200 million years ago and left by a small creature as it crossed a mud bank by a shallow pond in the desert landscape of the time. These are the only prints of their kind we know to have survived the aeons since.

There must have been large dinosaurs roaming Ireland; we just don't have the evidence. On the whole, Irish palaeontologists should consider themselves a little short-changed compared with their continental colleagues. England can claim at least two dozen species of dinosaur, including the 18 m tall *Cetiosaurus* and the named-for-a-reason *Megalosaurus*. It also had the 8 m high *Metriacanthosaurus*, whose fearsome appearance is done little justice by a name that translates as 'moderately-spined lizard'.

Scotland can claim a single dinosaur of its own, a *Saltopus* ('hopping foot') discovered in 1910. Although the bones found were fragmentary, a Triassic lizard believed to have been about the size of a cat, it may have been something similar to the creature that left its footprints in the Down mud all that time ago.

Understanding of what did once roam Ireland is relatively recent. In 1859, workers at a limestone quarry at Shandon, Co. Waterford chanced upon some large bones while digging through to a cave. Excited by the discovery, the workers paraded a particularly long bone through the streets of the town as the thighbone of a giant. Not wanting to let such a notable find go to waste, one of them loaded up a heap of bones and sold them to make bone dust.

Watching this unfold was a local postmaster and amateur naturalist, Edward Brenan. He went straight to the quarry, where he found that the rest of the bones had been broken up and carted away for use in repairing the roads. He requested that he be informed if they happened upon any more bones, and made the quarry workers promise to be more careful with them next time. Luckily, more were found and Brenan was summoned and he identified the large bones as being from a mammoth, and other bones as belonging to a bear, a horse, hare and reindeer. He gave a paper on his findings to the Royal Dublin Society, where he confidently informed the audience that the animals had, in all likelihood, died while huddling together in refuge from the biblical flood.

However ridiculous Brenan's conclusions may seem to us now, his findings marked the beginning of a new appreciation of the animals of ancient Ireland, although it was only through a widescale audit of bones—the Quatenary Fauna Project—in the 1990s that zoologists began to understand just what had been there to greet the first humans when they finally landed. So, while we have next to no evidence of the large animals roaming Ireland for hundreds of millions of years, we start to get a very good idea from about 45,000 years ago, when musk-ox and mammoth begin to show up on the record. We have found the bones of lemmings, reindeer, wolves, brown bears and spotted hyenas. The mammoths would have been made extinct in Ireland, it would seem, by environmental changes some time around 17,000 years ago and becoming globally extinct about 10,000 years ago. The island had only recently seen the last of the Irish Elk (neither an elk nor uniquely Irish) whose scientific name is the unambiguous *Megaloceros giganteus* because it stood 7 ft tall and had antlers that spanned 12 ft. The giant deer had possibly been a victim of the disappearance of the grasslands during a sudden, but severe, 600-year cold snap that interrupted the post-glacial warming.

However, wolves, lynx and brown bears remained in an Irish landscape that was heavily wooded with deciduous trees and which was now benefiting from the warming effect of the Gulf Stream off the west coast, which meant that a country whose midlands are at a similar latitude to Newfoundland to the west and Moscow to the east had become a lot more pleasant in the winter than either of those places.

The bounty of bones found in the Waterford cave survived because this would have been one of the few places relatively untouched by the ice sheets that occasionally stretched right the way down the country. The south of England escaped the worst of it, so again kept the best of the evidence. During some building work on the south side of London's Trafalgar Square in the 1950s, it was discovered that the area had once been a popular spot for rhinos, lions, hippopotamus and elephants.

Ten thousand years ago, Ireland was literally rising back from the Ice Age. During almost 60,000 years in deep freeze, the island had suffered particularly because it was stuck out in the frozen Atlantic. When the climate changed, it happened so abruptly that the temperature of the north Atlantic rose by a staggering 9 °F in only seven years, sending the ice into retreat. After that, the land could breathe again, having been crushed under several hundred metres of ice. It hasn't stopped bouncing back. Malin Head in Donegal is still rising about 2 mm a year as it recovers from the weight of ice that last touched it some 13,000 years ago.

So, at the tail end of the last Ice Age Ireland was a chilly but beautiful spot. Dense forests, punctuated by mountain ranges and occasional lakes, covered an island on which the peat bogs had yet to form. For a time, the ice had soaked up the seas, unveiling a landbridge between the south-east of Ireland and the south-west of Britain. Even as the ice sheets retreated and the released water brought a rise to sea levels, that landbridge remained until about

10,000 years ago. There is also believed to have been a short-lived bridge between Antrim and Scotland's Kintyre. These bridges brought several plant and animal species to Ireland in that time. It brought life to the island following thousands of years during which very little could survive. But the landbridge, it seems, did not bring humans.

The skies were busy with hawks, eagles and kestrels; the land and waters were rich with life. Yet, across the entire island there wasn't a single human footprint and there probably never had been. This despite the fact that 10,000 years ago, humans were scattered across the globe. There were probably five million people in all, descendants of a resilient species that had clung on through that recent Ice Age. During this time, the early western Europeans clung on in southern France and northern Spain, holding fast amid a climatic catastrophe that is estimated to have reduced their population to as little as only 9,000 people.

As the temperatures warmed, and the ice went north, so did the animals and the humans that hunted them. Modern humans trickled into Germany, Poland and eastern Europe. They went farther north into Denmark. They huddled by the snowline in Sweden and Norway. People were already in Africa, of course; they had been in Australia for at least 30,000 years; they were in North America. They had wandered across Europe, venturing farther and farther north. They went almost everywhere, in other words, except Ireland. This despite being firmly settled in Britain, which at that point was not an island. For centuries, if a person had wanted to move from France to Britain, all he had to do was walk across a forested and fertile plain that would later become the English Channel.

In fact, various evolutionary forms of humans had been in and out of Britain for about a quarter of a million years. They'd made it as far west as Wales. They may even have made it as far as the Irish Sea at times when it was a wide, verdant valley. They would have been on the doorstep of Ireland, but they never crossed the threshold. Or, if they did, we haven't found the evidence yet. This is a conundrum that's bothered archaeologists for a couple of centuries now.

Why it should have stayed empty remains something of a mystery, especially given how, for hundreds of thousands of years, Britain was comparatively overrun compared to Ireland. Connected by a wide landbridge to the north-west of the European continent, it had long offered easier access. It already hosted earlier human species, perhaps as far back as 700,000 years ago judging by the flint and bones found in sites in the south of England.

Palaeontologists know that 500,000 years ago one species, *Homo heidelbergensis* ('Heidelberg man') was definitely present. With a complex brain, it was a hunter, using stone blades to both kill and slash its meat. We know that it used relatively advanced blades and red ochre pigment as paint, even if we haven't found examples of any art it might have made with it. Some have theorised that it was the first human species to bury its dead and that it spoke a rudimentary language.

When Heidelberg man moved into Britain it was to take advantage of a warm climate, grassland and abundant prey—rhinos and bison among them—while trying to avoid becoming prey to the lions then roaming where London would later sprout. When palaeontologists found the bone—a lone tibia—that confirmed that Heidelberg man had been in Britain, it had been chewed upon by either a wolf or a hyena. So humans were clearly part of the food chain at the time, even if we can't be sure if the poor fellow was alive, dying or dead when he became a dog-snack.

Heidelberg man had wandered west from central Europe, where it had hunted and butchered large mammals including elephants. It is likely that—at either end of its place on the evolutionary chain at least—it lived alongside other human species. It also appears to have been relatively common because it has also been found in Germany (near the town of Heidelberg, hence its name), northern

Spain and Greece. Three sets of footprints pressed into volcanic ash in southern Italy, and the handprints of one who tried to avoid slipping, are believed to have been left behind some 345,000 years ago.

So, these early humans were widespread. They were next door. But they did not come to Ireland. Nor did Neanderthals—who may have evolved from Heidelberg man—make the journey, although they periodically arrived and left Britain by walking to it from the Continent. In fact, mankind, in one evolutionary form or other, made at least seven ultimately doomed attempts to settle in Britain and, while each was forced out by various onslaughts of ice, they all stayed around long enough to leave some evidence of their having been there.

Homo sapiens is believed to have first evolved in Africa some 200,000 years ago, reaching Asia and Europe about 40,000 years ago and working its way through the Continent until reaching Britain some 30,000 years ago. Its arrival is proven by radiocarbon dating of a skeleton found in Paviland, South Wales in 1823 by a Rev William Buckland. The reverend was a brilliant scientist, whose chief legacy to scientific research comes from his realisation that the stony white balls he was prodding were bits of ancient hyena dung and that fossilised faeces could offer vital clues to the past.

Unfortunately, his hunch on the Welsh skeleton proved some-what less accurate. Noting that the bones were coated in red ochre, he concluded that they were the remains of a Roman prostitute. Henceforth, the skeleton became known as the Red Lady of Paviland. It would be many years until we learned that it was neither a prostitute nor female. Instead, at 26,000 years old, it was the oldest formal burial of a *Homo sapiens* on these islands.

However, it would appear that, once again, these colonisers were forced out by the Ice Age. There is no evidence of human habitation of Britain between 21,000 and 15,000 years ago. Those who first returned there as the ice retreated would have been a hardy bunch, perhaps numbering a few hundred. And the change in the climate led to a yo-yoing of temperatures, so that what they had to contend with was another brief, but significant, cold snap about 11,000 years ago (scientists generally call it the Younger Dryas, but in Ireland it's known as the Nahanagan Stadial). The prevailing theory on why this happened is that the enormous quantities of cold water locked in the ice cap were released into the north Atlantic by the warming climate, only to disrupt the Gulf Stream and trigger a cold spell that lasted for about 1,000 years.

Nevertheless, pioneers crossed the landbridge connecting France and Britain and settled. This was the eighth wave of humans to attempt to colonise Britain, and the newly benign global climate meant that they would be the successful ones. The settlement of Britain, after many millennia of false starts, meant that Ireland was an obvious next step.

So, if they had made it all the way across the Continent and into Britain, why didn't they take the relatively short journey farther east into Ireland?

Maybe they did. As we've seen, nature has proven pretty good at disposing of the evidence, but occasionally something has popped up to add a little spice to this mystery. In 2008, archaeologists working on a site on a housing estate in Co. Down dug up a flint tool. Such finds are not unusual, but this one was 200,000 years old. It had been made before the Ice Age.

It was confirmed as a tool unique to the Middle Palaeolithic. The Palaeolithic refers the 'Old Stone Age', a period that covers some two and a half million years, several human species, and a lot of different tools. The Middle Palaeolithic began 300,000 years ago and lasted until about 35,000 years ago. Sometime during that period, someone, somewhere, sat down and chipped at a 7 cm piece of flint with a stone until he got a sharp edge to it. He wasn't even particularly good at it. It 'is not a very pretty artefact', observed Dr Farina Sternke, the consultant asked to establish its origin. 'The person that made it wasn't very proficient in what he or she was doing.'

Anyway, it was dropped or left behind, its owner never guessing that many millennia later it would be dug up on a housing estate in the north of Ireland and cause some excitement. Was this finally evidence that humans were in Ireland a couple of hundred thousand years ago after all?

Unfortunately not. It quickly became clear that the flint had been rolled to Ireland by ice or water, hitch-hiking to the North about 16,000 years ago. It may have come from Scotland or somewhere in the Irish Sea. But it wasn't Irish.

So, this critically panned but historically interesting bit of flint will go into the records alongside one found in a Drogheda quarry in 1968 and identified as waste from tool-making and struck by a technique commonly used by Stone Age man in England. It, too, had been rolled in such a way that it appears to have been picked up by the ice somewhere in the Irish Sea and carried to Ireland.

The only other evidence of early man being in Ireland turned out not to be all it seemed. In 1974, a hand axe was found in a defensive wall at the fort of Dún Aengus in Inishmore, off Galway. The tool clearly predates the known arrival of humans. Wherever it was from, though, the axe was not Irish. And however it ended up there remains something of a mystery, because it wasn't put there by a Stone Age Irishman. One crucial detail confirms that. As Frank Mitchell and Michael Ryan have explained in their indispensable *Reading the Irish Landscape*: 'A Palaeolithic hunter . . . could not have lost a very valuable tool in a crevice which did not yet exist.' It wasn't early man, they concluded, but probably a modern practical joker.

Such mysteries only put a focus on the larger one. If people were living close to Ireland, possibly as near as the Irish Sea at a time when much of its water had been sucked into the ice, then why didn't they keep going?

Two possible explanations have prevailed. The first is that humans *were* in Ireland, but that nature has proven expert at disposing of the evidence. There has been some speculation, for instance, that during various cold snaps humans might have been able to cling on to an unglaciated corner of the south of the otherwise frozen island, although some recent studies insist that little life could have held out. The most recent Ice Age was particularly catastrophic, driving animal species from the land and causing an astounding level of damage. The glaciers shaped the land, gouged out valleys and carried chunks of Scotland across to Ireland. And they did so over tens of thousands of years. Any traces of humanity were easily obliterated.

'The interesting thing is around this period of 30,000 to 40,000 years ago we have a hugely rich mammalian fauna in Ireland and there was no landbridge,' University College Cork archaeologist Professor Peter Woodman told the *Irish Times* in 2008.

We had hyenas and mammoths through to things like horse and red deer. Practically everything that was in Europe was in Ireland and there doesn't seem to have been a landbridge. Animals certainly get across, so why not humans? I think we place too much emphasis on water and the idea of having to have a dry land connection.

Nonetheless, the second, somewhat disappointing explanation is this: humans just didn't make it here for a long, long time.

Water was an obvious factor. People would have walked to Britain during those times when it was joined with Europe, but the opportunities to get to Ireland by foot were far more limited. And given that landbridges often formed during colder spells, when ice soaked up the water, Ireland's northerly position would not always have made it an enticing option.

Landbridges would also have formed as the ice retreated, when it was moving northwards but during which not enough water had been released to fill the Irish Sea. Ice was not so far south as to utterly discourage colonisation, nor so far north that the plains were once again flooded and Ireland returned to being an island.

These opportunities would have been short-lived, though, and would probably have coincided with the times when our ancestors were re-establishing themselves in the northern parts of the Continent. That they repeatedly had to leave Britain also shows how much more difficult it would have been for Heidelberg or Neanderthal people to move into Ireland and survive for any length of time.

And the problem for the modern humans was simple. Evolved as they were—no less intelligent, remember, than we are today— it took them a long time to get around to inventing something that would revolutionise the world: the boat.

In 1955, during the construction of a motorway that ran through a small bog in the Dutch village of Pesse, archaeologists dug up a hollowed out, 3 m long pine log. It was at least 9,500 years old and when it was in use it would have been able to take the weight of a man if it had been placed on water. This find was christened the Canoe of Pesse, and it could be the oldest known boat found. Presuming it was ever actually used as a boat. It may have been a coffin or maybe a trough. Whatever it was used for, at the very least it proves that at this point in history humans knew how to hollow a log that would, if desired, make for a half-decent boat.

From later in the Stone Age, we've found plenty of boats, including one in Denmark that was over 9 m long and capable of carrying at least six people and some equipment. Its sailors had used paddles, as the sail is only believed to have been invented about 5,000 years ago, and they had even kindled a fire at its rear.

The invention of the boat must have been a seismic evolution for Stone Age people. With it came previously unimaginable possibilities: fishermen could fish farther afield; rivers could be navigated; islands could be reached; and previously inaccessible lands could be colonised. Which is why it must have proved a watershed in Ireland's history, because sometime about 9,000 years ago, somewhere on the island, a boat pulled up on a beach and from it stepped perhaps the first people to ever touch Irish soil.

Where did they come from? It would also be common sense to expect that the first colonisers would take the shortest route here, which is among the reasons why the most obvious candidate has always been the north of Britain. It's also assumed that the north-east of Ireland was the landing point, because this is where the greatest concentration of early camps have since been found. About 9,000 years ago, the ice was still only retreating and the sea levels would have been lower than they are today. Not only would the two islands have been closer together, but in clear weather Stone Age adventurers would have been able to island-hop from the west coast of Scotland to the north-east of Ireland without ever losing sight of the mainland.

That presumes, of course, that they came from Scotland. They may have come from Wales, aided by the way the narrow channel to the north of the Irish Sea and the wide channel to the south would have provided powerful currents.

They may have come from the south-west of England, from where the south-east of Ireland was eminently reachable even if it didn't offer too many islands along the way.

They could have gone from Cornwall to Antrim, stopping at the Isle of Man along the way, because it forms a hub in the centre of the Irish Sea on which tidal flows are centred.

The first Irish may have come from Denmark, given that the early Danes not only had the boat-building technology but had already used it to get to England. Irish Stone Age sites also have similarities with those in Denmark.

Or they may have originally worked their way up the Atlantic coast from Spain, which had acted as a refuge for people as they migrated away from the ice sheets.

At which point we should stop and acknowledge that to assign these people any nationality is an obviously anachronistic exercise, given that there were no Danes, Spanish, Scottish, English or Irish at the time. They would have belonged to small settlements and recognised loyalty only to their kin, making occasional contact with other settlements to trade, or sometimes to fight. Instead, in academic terms, the first 'Irish' are broadly considered Mesolithic people, literally 'Middle Stone Age' who succeeded the 'Old Stone Age' Palaeolithic about 12,000 years ago, with the clear distinction between the two being in the kinds of tools each used. By the time they reached Ireland, the Mesolithic people had already spread across the globe, with the total population of the planet at the time being about five million.

Despite the catch-all term, there were variations across cultures in how they cut their tools, buried their dead and lived. For instance, the Mesolithic people who came to Ireland did not make pottery, even though the Jōmon people of Japan had already been doing that for several thousand years. You can tell a surprising amount about a people from their pots because it's likely that pottery was something that developed only in cultures that didn't move around too much. The Jōmon were relatively sedentary, but the hunter-gatherers who arrived in Ireland would have moved depending on the seasons or prey. Pottery was too easily broken to carry around.

Why did people come to Ireland in the first place? We can only guess. People have always migrated for a variety reasons, whether it's to follow food, resources or their own curiosity. The first Irish may have been forced out of their homeland by the competition for resources. They may have been tempted by the relative tranquillity of Ireland's east coast when compared to a Scottish west coast that is open to the Atlantic. They may have been adventurous, having eyed Ireland from the islands of Scotland and wondered what might be there.

Or there is the possibility that the first Irish were actually those who had been cast out of their settlements for some wrongdoing or other, or because they lost out in a power struggle. Throughout history, colonists of new lands have not always wanted to leave their homes in the first place.

The first parties might not have stayed, but, having landed and in a corner of the world where room and food was plentiful and the raw material for their tools was literally falling at their feet, returned to their home settlement and prepared to move for good.

When they arrived in Ireland, they would have had just about everything they needed to survive. These were hunter-gatherers, not farmers. Agriculture was only being developed in the Fertile Crescent that sweeps around the Middle East and was thousands of years away from reaching Ireland. What the first Irish required was fresh water, fishing grounds and animals to hunt. They would have gradually noticed that there was not much in the way of bigger animals—no cattle or elk—but there was smaller prey.

Most importantly, if they were going to be able to hunt at all, they needed the raw materials for their weapons and in the north-east of Ireland they would have been delighted to realise that flint—the stuff of their blades—was so plentiful that they could scoop it up by the armful. It could hardly be considered the most glamorous of stones, but for a couple of million years flint was about the most important influence on the development of humanity.

Hard, but brittle, it develops as nodular seams in chalk, resembling raisins in an uncooked cake. About 200 million years ago, Ireland and its neighbours had emerged from epochs underwater almost entirely covered in a layer of chalk about 100 m thick. Britain has a reminder of this in the White Cliffs of Dover, but there is so little evidence left of it in Ireland that to believe it, Frank Mitchell observed, 'almost requires an act of geological faith'.

That chalk was in the final stages of disappearing by the time people landed here, but in the north-east it was being sheared from the mountains in such amounts that little effort would have been needed to harvest the flint. Tools would have been made from other materials—wood, bone, antler and shell—but it is the stone tools that have survived the millennia in greater numbers.

At Mount Sandel, just outside Coleraine, Co. Derry flints had been surfacing for about a century before, in 1973, a team of archaeologists arrived on a routine excavation on land that was being prepared for a new housing estate. Led by Professor Peter Woodman, they arrived with fears that whatever artefacts might have been there had already been destroyed by extensive plough-ing. Thankfully, they had not. Instead, they had discovered the oldest settlement then found in Ireland.

Woodman's team found hazelnut shells, eel and other fish bones. There were the charred seeds of water lilies, which would have been part of the diet. There were goshawk bones—a bird of prey later made extinct in Ireland until a return in later years. There was evidence that hares and wild pigs had been killed there. There were tool-making areas in which blades that hunted, skinned and cut the meat would have been made. They also found tools made of chert, a stone not found in the north-east, so when-ever people were living at Mount Sandel, they were already in contact with settlements from the south of the island, which would have relied on that stone.

The settlement itself was in a naturally widened hollow, which is not surprising given that their tools were inadequate for clearing trees in any large-scale way. There is evidence of seven structures, six of which were round, about 6 m in diameter with a hollow at the centre that would have acted as a hearth. They would have been built by spearing saplings into the ground, and bending them until they joined at the centre. They would have been covered in either animal hide or a thatch of lighter branches, to give shelter, but with a hole at the top to allow smoke out. Around the hearth were small stakeholes, the evidence of a rack that had been used for cooking.

Along with the chert tools, flint was also found—largely waste discarded by the process of making the tools—and there were some completed tools too. The flint would have come from the Co. Antrim coast, some distance away. But the site also threw up a new mystery, which was the presence of polished stone axes that weren't supposed to have been introduced until about 3,000 years later when the first farmers arrived.

While many Stone Age groups would have been nomadic, the inhabitants of Mount Sandel appear to have spent most of the year at the site: the salmon bones suggest that they spent their summers here at least; eel bones and hazelnuts that they stayed during the autumn; and the youth of the slaughtered pigs that they were still there late in the winter.

Radiocarbon dating would later pinpoint the settlement as being from between 7010 to 6490 BC. It was a find so significant that the earliest colonisers are now labelled as 'Sandelian' to distinguish them from the people and cultures that would follow later.

Although a vital glimpse of the Early Irish, Mount Sandel is not evidence of the earliest colonisers. While many of their tools were similar to those being used by Mesolithic peoples across northern Europe, some were actually unique to Ireland. The needle-points they used for making clothes or for stitching together the coverings for their homes are not found anywhere else. It means that when Mount Sandel was occupied, people had been in Ireland long enough to both spread through the island, and to develop indigenous techniques. Whoever they were, these were not the pioneers.

Of course, you wait for one Mesolithic settlement and then two come along at once. In 1977, four years after the Mount Sandel findings, Lough Boora in Co. Offaly was being drained so its peat could be harvested. It revealed the remnants of a camp that had once been on a peninsula of a fossilised shoreline. Radiocarbon dating subsequently dated it to having been occupied at the same time as the settlement at Mount Sandel.

Unlike Mount Sandel, this seems unlikely to have been a semi-permanent settlement. The remnants of campfires were found, but no huts. A large number of tools were found, although none were of flint. Again, there were clues about the diet of its inhabitants as the hearths contained young wild pig, hares and, possibly, duck bones. The bones of a dog were also believed to be among the debris, suggesting that the hunters had domesticated the animal.

In the space of only a few years, the understanding of the early Irish had grown enormously. Yet, there are large gaps in our knowledge. Much of what is known of these early people comes from the discovery of material at a scattering of sites that stretch down the island, always around water, as far as Ferriter's Cove in Co. Kerry, usually close to sea level, but with the bulk huddled in the north-east corner.

However, the acidic nature of the soil in the north-east set about eating away at human bones, meaning burials are almost entirely lacking (although cremated remains were found in Co. Limerick in 2001). So, when trying to guess how these first Irish lived, a certain amount of conjecture is needed, and a lot of help from sites found in other parts of the world.

It's uncertain what culture they would have brought with them, but it seems likely that it would have been similar to that found at Star Carr, a Mesolithic site in Yorkshire that was in use for a 350-year period over 10,000 years ago. Among its most famous relics is a set of perforated antlers that would have been used as a headpiece, maybe for ritualistic purposes or perhaps as a hunting disguise.

The early settlers in Ireland would have brought medical knowledge, such as it was, although because we don't have any burials to go by, and they are very rare elsewhere in Europe, we don't know what their life expectancy would have been although there is speculation that it may have been as low as the mid-twenties. We can be sure, though, that infant mortality would have been extremely high. In such a society, it's likely that women would have carried children from a young age, with puberty possibly the focus of certain rituals, as is common in most cultures up to today. They may have married in formal ceremonies, the arrangements being made for kinship purposes or possibly as a form of bonding between tribes.

And such inter-tribal contracts may have been necessary, in that warfare between groups, perhaps triggered by rights to hunting grounds, may have occasionally broken out. Across Europe, Stone Age skeletons have been found with arrows embedded in them, skulls crushed, flint knives in their throats. Around 8,500 years ago, at an ancient village in southern Germany, 38 people—mainly women and children—were massacred, probably while the men were away hunting. Warfare is too common an occupation for it to have been entirely absent among the early Irish, where blades were being perfected at the same time as hunting grounds were being claimed.

When burying their dead, the early Irish would have had some form of belief system. The red ochre that gave the Red Lady of Paviland its name was undoubtedly put there as part of some ritual, and the skeleton was also surrounded by grave goods including periwinkle shells and ivory. That site is 26,000 years old, making it the oldest ceremonial burial in western Europe. The earliest known cemetery in Britain, a cave in Somerset that contained 21 bodies and was marked with crosses, dates back 10,000 years.

Would they have spoken a language? Almost certainly. Even Neanderthals, by then long extinct, may have spoken, although there is no scientific consensus on this because while it has been confirmed that they shared a 'language gene' found in modern humans, their anatomy would have limited their vocal range.

Homo sapiens, with its fully-formed voice box, was able to speak from the off. If it was the first to develop language, why it would have evolved is still open to argument: it may have been an evolutionary adaptation, or it may have simply been a happy by-product of some other development. There are a great deal of theories surrounding all of this, many of them carrying some onomatopoetically amusing names, such as the pooh-pooh theory, the bow-wow theory and the ding-dong theory.

None of them tells us *when* exactly humans developed complex language. It may have developed slowly as we became used to the advantages of a voice box. Or it could have happened immediately upon the arrival of modern man, perhaps explaining just why it was that we became the dominant hominid species so quickly (planning a hunt or an attack or anything at all is much easier when everyone can talk to each other). When we look at the sophistication of many of the tools that are dated to the Mesolithic period, we can see that language may have been needed to pass on these skills from generation to generation.

What language this was, we don't know. It may have been a locally specific version of a Proto-World language, a root of all current tongues, which some linguists believe was common. But it was not a written language, and there are no confirmed descendants of it today.

The first people would have brought all of these aspects of their culture, just as surely as they brought the tools and skills, which were passed on, through subsequent generations. Nevertheless, it seems that the island became insular enough that, about 8,000 years ago, the Irish developed their own distinctive style of tool-making, as seen at Mount Sandel. The only parallels, curiously, are found on the Isle of Man. That small island, sandwiched between Britain and Ireland, would be a regular stop-off for Irish from the earliest days and for thousands of years to come. Yet, Ireland was not entirely cut off from influences or people, something which is driven home by how, about 6,000 years ago, someone became the island's first farmer.

————

The impact of farming on a landscape cannot be underestimated. From the moment it arrived in Ireland, several thousand years after it had first evolved in the Middle East, it marked an environmental watershed: the clearing of the forests that had dominated the island, the arrival of new species, the settling down of the people and the development of new technologies. It had such an impact that, in contrast to the comparably ephemeral imprint left by the Mesolithic people, the physical evidence of this new way of life is still dotted around the Irish countryside today.

This culture, and its people, are referred to as Neolithic—a 'New' Stone Age people to complete the troika begun by 'Old' Palaeolithic and 'Middle' Mesolithic. The Neolithic period in Ireland lasted for a couple of thousand years from about 4500 BC, although until about 4000 BC Mesolithic man was still clinging on to his outdated ways, a spell referred to as the Later Mesolithic, or sometimes the Ultimate Mesolithic.

How did farming get to Ireland? We can only guess. It may have come here with new people, triggered by a wave of mass migration in western Europe. It may have been introduced by only a few settlers whose ideas were picked up by the locals. Or it may have been imported by Irish traders bringing back ideas and technology they had seen abroad. There would have been trade between Ireland and Britain, in the likes of cured fish, animal skins and tools. It's hard to imagine that, among all those traders going back and forth across the Irish Sea, there weren't entrepreneurial sorts who could spot the benefits of farming.

To understand how it might have happened, we have to return to the boat. This technology had gradually developed during the Mesolithic era. From an archaeological record that is scant to say the least, the earliest Irish log boat—in fact, the earliest shipwreck of any kind in Ireland—is a Mesolithic log boat found (by Peter Woodman) in Lough Neagh that has been dated to 5300 BC. Six metres long, it had a boulder at its stern, just as has been found in other Mesolithic log boats. Quite why the stone was there—for ballast, or simply to stop the boat from floating away—remains something of a mystery.

Boats made with planks were still a couple of thousand years away from being developed, but Mesolithic boats covered in hides were capable of tackling decent journeys while carrying substantial loads. Even then, we have to assume that not everyone could take to the seas. The boat would have been an exceptionally complex bit of equipment, requiring skill to both make and use. A Neolithic sailor wouldn't have been able to just push the boat off a beach and point it in a certain direction any more than someone would today. They would have needed an understanding of the weather, tides, some basic astronomical knowledge, and been able to keep a steady course.

There is, as ever, a certain amount of guesswork as to where farming—or farmers—came from although north-west Britain would be a likelihood given how its islands acted as stepping stones to the north-east coast of Ireland. However, the earliest domesticated animals that have been found anywhere in Britain or Ireland are the sheep and cattle of Ferriter's Cove, Co. Kerry, from about 4500 BC. To confuse matters somewhat, this is considered to be a Mesolithic settlement, which suggests that the animals arrived here before the farming techniques. It may be that Ireland imported domesticated animals from Britain, because, unlike the neighbours, the island had few large mammals of its own, although pigs may have been domesticated from our own native species.

Anyway, as farming became established in Ireland, these Neolithic people began to clear the land, hacking at trees with their stone axes, and using clearance methods that, curiously, appear to have originated from techniques used north of the Alps rather than along the western Atlantic seaboard. The Neolithic farmers also introduced cereals—barley, wheat—which did not grow wild in Ireland. And, as proof that their wandering was coming to an end, pottery finally made its debut.

As we have seen, around this time cattle were also introduced to Ireland, as well as domesticated sheep and goats (which were not native to Britain or Ireland). It is hard, from this perspective, to imagine the inconvenience and downright unpleasantness of taking farm animals across the Irish Sea, in a relatively rudimentary hide-covered boat. It seems logical to believe that they took calves rather than fully matured cattle. But it was necessary, because cattle were not native to Ireland—unlike Britain, which had the auroch, a wild species that was once common across Europe, but eventually became extinct in 1627 when the last of them died in Poland. Horses weren't introduced until 2000 BC, and the island only saw its first cat another couple of thousand years after that.

Neolithic people began to establish permanent settlements, such as one excavated at Lough Gur, Co. Limerick. Situated on fertile soil, by a lake surrounded by sheltered valleys, it was a good place to live and farm (it still is) and its buildings were round and rectangular. The latter houses would have had three aisles running through them, with the centre aisle possibly used during the day, while the edges were used for storage or sleeping. In the circular huts, meanwhile, there were holes in the ground from which mud had been taken to form the walls and the holes were then used as rubbish pits.

In the area of Lough Gur, archaeologists also found the grave of a 14-year-old boy. Buried 1 m down, he was lying towards his left side, his legs slightly drawn up towards his chest. There was a bowl at his head. At another part of the site, two children—aged perhaps five and six—were buried together by a house, in a similar position, with a piece of pottery found with the younger child.

Even before it was excavated Lough Gur was already a really useful place for our understanding of Neolithic culture as it was also home to something which didn't need to be dug up to be discovered. Because close by is a rather extraordinary feature known as the Grange stone circle. Here, 113 stones are arranged in a near-perfect ring, and its entrance has tall stones that are mirrored by those directly opposite. These align perfectly with the midsummer moon. It is an evocative reminder of something else the Neolithic culture brought to Ireland. At a time when death was commonplace across all ages, the people began to bury the bodies in a formal way, and they did so in an increasingly spectacular fashion.

The Mesolithic people would have been less inclined towards formal burial because it tends to have developed where people stayed put and developed organised communities. And once they started, they really went for it. In contrast to the paucity of Mesolithic burial sites, archaeologists have found Neolithic bodies and graves everywhere. Something like 1,400 Neolithic tombs still exist in the Irish landscape. There may be more waiting to be found. And there have certainly been hundreds destroyed over recent centuries.

Neolithic people tend to have been interred in one of four types of tombs (court, portal, wedge and passage), and each is generally clustered in particular parts of the island. For instance, most of the almost 400 court tombs are found in the northern half of Ireland, and it is presumed that it's unlikely to be mere coincidence that there are a lot of these tombs in Scotland.

The 150 portal tombs (commonly known as dolmens, and which, roughly explained, have tall stones either side of a straight chamber, with a single slab sometimes blocking the entrance) are mostly in Ulster, but they're also dotted along the east coast as far south as Waterford. And they are similar to tombs found in Wales and Cornwall. Wedge tombs (as the name suggests, they are wedge-shaped) are concentrated largely in the south of the country, although what makes them particularly interesting is that there are no wedge tombs at all in Britain. Some believe that there may be prototypes in Brittany, but it is possible that they were a purely Irish development.

Finally, we come to passage tombs, which tend to be on higher ground and grouped together. They gained their name because they feature a passage that leads to a chamber. These are the tombs that most modern Irish would have little trouble picturing, because all they have to do is close their eyes and think of the winter solstice sun flooding Newgrange. It is the Co. Meath tomb that also gives us the most obvious reminder that the Neolithic people brought not just rituals but some really wonderful buildings to conduct them at.

The thing about Newgrange is that, while it may be a star attraction, it is far from being alone in the area. The area of Brú na Bóinne—the bend of the River Boyne—is littered with passage tombs. Alongside Newgrange are the tombs of Knowth and Dowth. Curiously, if you stand at the top of any one of them, you can see the other two. Nor was Newgrange alone in being treated a little roughly by later generations. To the west of Newgrange are two mounds, referred to as K and L. In the nineteenth century, someone operated a lime-kiln in the cruciform tomb at mound L, doing ferocious damage in the process.

Many of the area's passage tombs have been damaged over the years. We get a reminder that graffiti is hardly a modern invention, because sometime between AD 700 and 750 a person, or people, got to work carving 20 names into the stones at Knowth. Those scribblings go alongside one of the most significant collections of Stone Age art known anywhere. They demonstrate that with the Neolithic people developed a style of art that is still recognised now, and which is often mistaken for, and appropriated as, Celtic. The style may have indeed been peculiarly Irish, though. Across the island, there are examples of a style that may have been picked up from either Brittany or Iberia, but spirals seem to be a particularly Irish flourish. Some of those found are clearly of importance in rituals or celebrations. Some are clearly not. 'There are many items that can only be looked upon as doodles or graffiti executed by prentice hands in moments of idleness,' wrote Michael O'Kelly, 'so carelessly are they done in comparison with the best formal work.' Like that poorly cut flint found in Down recently, it's chastening to realise that the precious work handed down through history may have been done by a bored student or cack-handed amateur.

The designs carved on the stones at Meath's tombs would have been made using stone tools, and seem likely to have been drawn only after the stones were dragged there. The carving on the entrance of Newgrange is considered to be one of the greatest surviving pieces of prehistoric art.

And what convinced people to drag 200,000 tonnes of stone from a riverbank a mile away to make Newgrange, and to build all the other tombs scattered about the area? O'Kelly believed that they may have been built, not by large colonising forces, but by small groups encouraged by preachers who would explain the idea and then leave the builders to take it from there. This would, he said, account for the variety in the types of tombs, the way that 'local variations and exuberances easily came into being'.

Whatever compelled them to go to such lengths to build Newgrange, and its companion tombs, with astronomical precision, the results are impressive. The area, and the Neolithic monuments, tombs, bodies and farmsteads scattered across Ireland, give the kind of insight into the early farmers that archaeologists would dearly love to have into the lives of those who arrived here before them.

Yet, in recent years archaeology has found itself able to learn things it could never previously have known. DNA evidence is giving us a glimpse into not just the family tree, but the depth of its roots. Scientific work has on the one hand shown us that the mystery will not be solved easily because we are as yet unable to guess with any confidence where the original Irish came from. There has been a small but significant amount of work done in trying to identify just where our later ancestors migrated from and there is hope that some day archaeologists might get a decently preserved body from which they'll be able to glean some information.

As it happens, by looking at the genetic inheritance of the Irish and tracing it back a few thousand years at least, we have begun to throw some light on one of the great talking points of Irish history. This is something of a relief. You might presume that because we know more about the Neolithic than the Mesolithic, then we should know even more about the people who came after them. But what followed was supposed to be the Celtic invasion of Ireland. And things really aren't that simple at all.

Chapter 2

THE DISAPPEARING PEOPLE: THE CELTS

Johann Georg Ramsauer was a decent manager of his local salt mine, but not so much that history would have remembered him for that. Luckily, when not busy with his career, Ramsauer was something of an amateur antiquarian. So, the day he realised that one of the greatest archaeological finds of his time was buried right beneath his feet must have been a very good day indeed.

The small town of Hallstatt, western Austria is a spectacular spot, hugging the edge of an Alpine lake, the mountains crowded behind it. Still, prehistoric people wouldn't have moved there just for the view. The salt has been the lure for 7,000 years, leaving the town with ancient mineshafts and giving it its name (*hall* is the German word for salt). And it's left something else of extraordinary value, because if you ever want to guarantee a corpse a certain level of immortality, then burying it in salty earth is a pretty good way to go about it.

Well before Ramsauer began working at the mine, Bronze Age dead had been poking through the earth, but these 'men of the salt', as they were called, would be reburied, having first been pilfered for any burial goods. In 1846, however, seven bodies were found during some gravel mining at the base of the salt mountain. We should be thankful that Ramsauer knew just what to do with them.

At the time, archaeology was just developing as a science, so it was still a time of amateur antiquarians: gentlemen hobbyists whose enthusiasm didn't always match their knowledge. Finds could be ruined as quickly as they were discovered. A person might pick something up, examine it carefully and then put it in their pocket and walk away. Ramsauer wasn't that kind of antiquarian. A pioneer, his techniques were careful and his observations detailed. He made sure that one of his miners, Isidor Engel, reproduced them in vivid watercolour. The results are a meticulous and evocative tableaux of skeletons resting with the goods or animals they were to take with them to the next life.

Over the next couple of decades, and using his own money, Ramsauer oversaw the excavation of almost 1,000 graves, unearthed 20,000 objects and continued to run the salt mine. And, somehow, he still found time to marry three women and sire 22 children. It was a full life.

Today, Hallstatt is a village of only 1,000 people and it has been estimated that the number of buried bodies could outnumber them eight times over. Even now, most of our knowledge about the site is thanks to Ramsauer. In all, only about 1,300 graves have been excavated, but the historical rewards have been rich. Archaeologists have found swords, spears, daggers, helmets, armour, chariots, horse harnesses, pottery and metal vessels. They have dug up the fur caps, shoes and woollen clothes that give us an idea of what prehistoric miners wore while digging through a frozen mountain, as well as the leftover food discarded by them as they did it. There are the pinewood chips that were lit to illuminate the mineshafts, and leather baskets used to carry the salt. It is here that we can find the oldest wooden staircase in Europe, which dates back 3,300 years.

A decade after Hallstatt began coughing up its secrets, an antiquarian, Hansli Kopp, spotted a couple of submerged stakes in a shallow part of the waters of Switzerland's Lake Neuchâtel, by the town of La Tène. Kopp rooted around between the stakes and pulled up an Iron Age weapon. He put his hand in and found another, and another, until he had 40 in all. Word spread of his great discovery. People came from all over to loot the lake.

It was soon realised that the La Tène finds were similar not only to archaeological sites found in France but also to those found in Hallstatt, even though these stretched back to an earlier period. Together, these finds were to prove so important that they gave their names to entire cultures. They had provided graves, art, tools and weapons, and they had presented them in a neat chronology. Most crucially, this seemed to be the great confirmation of something that people had long speculated about—that there was once a great Celtic race that stretched across Europe. Where there were Celts there were La Tène influences, which itself seemed to be a development from the Hallstatt cultures. This was a spectacular time for archaeology. People had been looking for evidence of this grand Celtic civilisation and here, in central Europe, they believed they had found it.

If only it had been so straightforward.

———

Few historical orthodoxies have been so quickly overhauled and reversed in so short a space of time as the story of the Celts. They were, until relatively recently, confidently believed to have been a great race that had emerged in central Europe during the Iron Age, and then spread outwards until they settled and conquered the lands and islands to the far west, where the remnants hold fast to the culture's language, art, genes and collective identity.

Today, there is no longer any real academic appetite for labelling the masses of Iron Age Europe as Celtic. 'Celtic' is considered an artistic style instead of a civilisation. There is certainly a shared style that flourished in Iron Age Europe, from about 800 BC, but it is not enough for us to describe it as belonging to any one great civilisation. Those who continue using the term treat the Celts more as a style, a way of life, a linked set of languages, rather than any specific peoples; that even if there wasn't a Celtic race in the past, there is a Celtic identity now, which is worth acknowledging and examining. There are those who feel it would be better left behind, that if we were to start from scratch the Celts would have no place in the new narrative of European history. It is, they say, a tenuous historical idea. And it gets more tenuous with every step you take towards Ireland.

Ireland as a Celtic nation—in the traditional sense—is no longer a popular idea. Which is tough news to get across to people. Souvenir shops market the idea of Celtic Ireland through their tea towels and T-shirts, not only because the tourists want to believe in it, but because the Irish believe in it themselves. Ireland considers itself part of a confederation of Celts that stretches along the Atlantic seaboard, with Scotland to the north and Brittany to the east. Yet, much of that identity has been constructed only in the past couple of hundred years. In fact, until the early twentieth century the individual nations actually resisted the idea of a pan-Celticism.

That the Hallstatt and La Tène finds were filed under Celtic is a case of using evidence to fulfil assumptions. But from its earliest days, Celticism meant different things depending on the perspective, and it continues to offer a lot of confusion. To linguists it refers to the related languages of the western fringes of Europe. To archaeologists, it means loosely related finds from across the Continent. To the tourist industries of Scotland, Wales and Ireland, it means money. To a great many historians, it means a headache.

That it should have happened this way is often blamed on Edward Lhuyd, the Welshman whose descriptions of Newgrange have proved so enduring. Born in 1660, Lhuyd's career as a botantist, geographer, fossil hunter and all-round antiquarian was deeply impressive. He trained quarry workers to identify fossils, and with the help of his friend Isaac Newton published a ground-breaking and practical field guide to English fossil finds, even if his understanding of how the fossils ended up where they did was forgivably naïve. Sea mist, he explained, was impregnated with the 'seed' of marine animals, which fell as rain on top of the ground where it germinated. This explained the number of fossilised shells found well away from the seashore.

Lhuyd was so dedicated to his profession that he literally worked himself to death, expiring in 1709 as a result of the damp in his room at the Ashmoleum Museum, Oxford University, where he worked and preferred to sleep rather than waste time going home.

Much of Lhuyd's unpublished work was later destroyed in a fire, but by the time of his death he had finished the book that would be his most influential. It was *Archaeologia Britannica: An Account of the Languages, Histories and Customs of Great Britain, from Travels through Wales, Cornwall, Bas-Bretagne, Ireland and Scotland*. Printed in 1707, it included valuable descriptions and observations of various monuments across these regions. It was Lhuyd who introduced the idea of the languages of these islands being Celtic. Why did he choose this term? Simon James, in his iconoclastic *The Atlantic Celts: Ancient People or Modern Invention?*, wonders if it is because Gallic (after the Gauls of France) was too strongly attached to the French, who were then the enemies of the English. Whatever the reason, it was to prove seminal.

Lhuyd was actually following in the footsteps of a French contemporary, Paul Yves Pezron, whose work he championed. Pezron had written a book, which was translated into English in 1706 as *The antiquities of nations; more particularly of the Celtae or Gauls, taken to be originally the same people as our ancient Britains*. The bit about the 'Britains' was added on for the translation of a creative story of the supposed common ancestry of the Welsh and Bretons, who, it was explained, could trace their family tree back to biblical roots. It's worth noting that he made no mention whatsoever of Ireland.

To Pezron's imagination, though, Lhuyd brought scholarly expertise. Within a short space of time, the word 'Celtic' was being ascribed not just to languages but to national identities and archaeological monuments.

During the seventeenth and eighteenth centuries, the Scots, Welsh and Irish went on separate trajectories, essentially moulding the idea to suit their individual needs. The idea that there was a Celtic nation, separated by sea but joined by culture, was not at all popular at first. In fact, there was strong resistance to the very idea among each of the nations, and it is something which only developed in the twentieth century.

In Ireland, as in other 'Celtic' areas, the irony is that the journey towards becoming Celtic began with the term as a form of abuse, as an indication of otherness, of barbarians, of a Celtic Fringe. The theory was floating about throughout the sixteenth and seventeenth centuries, when complex and often confused attempts were made to establish the origins of the races of Europe.

Through the Celts, however, the Irish began to view themselves not as the savages on the edges of Europe, but as survivors of an enlightened, advanced, glorious Celtic civilisation. Early proponents were men such as Charles O'Connor, Charles Vallancey and Sylvester O'Halloran, who were enthusiastic amateurs keen to revive the history and spirit of Celtic Ireland. These Celtic ideas, however, were not developed for revolutionary reasons. Many of its champions were Trinity scholars, clergymen, lawyers and country gentlemen. Charles Vallancey, for instance, was a high-ranking officer in the British army.

And what a place the Celtic civilisation had been: a land that truly was busy with saints and scholars, that was developed, learned, peaceful, self-governing and artistic. Proponents attempted to audit and rescue legal documents, folklore and poetry and wrote impassioned works, but were not attempting to cleave division between Britain and Ireland, but trying to place Celtic Ireland at the centre of European culture. They saw greatness in the growing British Empire and wanted Ireland to be a partner rather than a mere subject.

During the nineteenth century, however, Celtic civilisation was seen as offering an alternative to the English values being imposed on the Irish. It proved very attractive for those who saw ethnic difference as a way towards political separation, and a cultural revival was created on the reconstructed history of the Gaelic Irish.

It drew on cultural memory, which was clearly less reliable than historical evidence, but useful all the same because it was easier to piece together a history that suited the needs. Through it was this sense of grasping the definition of 'other' and transforming it into 'better'. Political and cultural nationalism became entwined, making a powerful combination. From a mythical past there was the promise of an independent future.

It would be used by revolutionaries, and would remain integral to the early part of the Irish State, inspiring an identity that was considered both pure and marketable. And despite a slow start, it did eventually become allied with the broader idea of pan-Celticism, a shared identity of Celtic races resurgent despite all.

Which is why it has been tough to persuade the Irish—and the Scottish, Welsh, Bretons, Manx and Cornish—that the most cherished element of their identity is built on a grand piece of self-deception. But the term 'Celtic' has become so grubby in some quarters that it's not unusual to now see it referred to as 'the C-word'.

———

Yet, there was once a people called, either by themselves or others, the Celts or *Keltoi*, because the ancient Greeks occasionally wrote about them, and the Roman Empire described itself as fighting a war against them. Whether each was talking about the same people, though, is unknown. Still, it's clear that when the Romans took on the race they believed to be the Celts, they were not charging at an invisible army.

It was the Greeks who first mentioned the Celts. In 517 BC, a philosopher, Hecataeus of Miletus, wrote an account of the known world at the time—although his known world was largely confined to the lands around the Mediterranean. His account has survived only as quotes in other works, but from those we know that he mentioned the Keltoi who lived in southern France, close to modern-day Marseille, in a region surrounding a Greek colony established there. What that tribe called themselves, we can't be sure, and Keltoi may have been a Greek word that stuck.

Another Greek, Herodotus, mentioned them the following century, writing that they were a people of western Europe and that the River Danube rose in their territory. Just to confuse things for subsequent historians, the Greeks then proceeded to use the term 'Celts' to generally describe the people of central and western Europe. This gives us an early hint that it may have been used as a collective term to denote the masses who lived beyond the bounds of the classical world.

Anyway, the people of central Europe are described as spreading outwards due to a wave of migration, which Roman historians—writing a few hundred years after the event itself—blamed on overpopulation. Whatever the reason, we know that they migrated as far south as the Po Valley, which is when the Romans began to take a particular interest in them. The Celts proved troublesome, sacking Delphi and besieging Rome. They travelled farther into the Balkans, into Transylvania. They took advantage of the instability in Macedonia that followed the death of Alexander the Great in 323 BC. They moved into Asia Minor (roughly modern-day Turkey). And, occasionally, they proved useful to have fighting on the Romans' side, such as when some of these Celts acted as mercenaries in the Second Punic War (probably the only Punic War the average person on the street would know anything whatsoever about, because this was the campaign during which Hannibal crossed the Alps).

Roman writings add some colour to this description of the hordes flooding south towards Rome after 440 BC. They are said to have laid siege to Rome for seven months until a thousand pounds of gold was mustered to pay them to go away. Legend has it that the deal came with some nervy moments. As the gold was being weighed, the Romans claimed that the Celts were cheating them by using faulty scales, and the Celtic leader, a fellow called Brennus, is then described as throwing his sword onto the balance and rubbing things in by mocking: 'Woe to the defeated!'

For a really meaty description, though, there is Julius Caesar's writings on the Gallic Wars of the last century BC. The Celts appear in the first line.

> All Gaul is divided into three parts, one of which the Belgae inhabit, the Aquitani another, those who in their own language are called Celts, in ours Gauls, the third. All these differ from each other in language, customs and laws. The river Garonne separates the Gauls from the Aquitani; the Marne and the Seine separate them from the Belgae.

At which point, you might expect him to talk up the prowess of the Celts. Not so. The fiercest race of all, Caesar explained, was the Belgian, as they 'are the bravest, because they are furthest from the civilization and refinement of [our] Province, and merchants least frequently resort to them, and import those things which tend to effeminate the mind'.

That Caesar referred to both Gauls and Celts as meaning the same thing yet again illustrates the confusion sown, and modern historians have tended to treat the Gauls as being almost inter-changeable with the Celts. Even by the time that Caesar mentioned them, the Gauls had been popping up in accounts for about three centuries, but historians think that the distinction may have been between the general masses of the 'Celtic' population of Europe, compared with the Gallic tribes who emigrated south and south-east and against whom the Romans went to war until finally defeating them in 51 BC.

During that same century, a Sicilian-born, Greek historian, Diodorus Siculus, took on the not inconsiderable task of writing a history of everything. By the time he had 40 books under his belt, he had still only made it to the beginning of the seven-year-long Gallic Wars, and while it's possible that he kept going for several volumes and that they have since disappeared over time, it's considered more likely that he simply ran out of energy before he could go any further.

Diodorus' descriptions are vivid to the point of being caricature.

> The Gauls are tall of body, with skin moist and white; their hair is blond not only by nature but also because they practise to increase artificially the peculiar nature of their colouring. Some of them shave off their beards but others let them grow moderately: the nobles shave their cheeks but let their moustaches grow freely so as to cover their mouths. Therefore, when they are eating, the moustaches become mixed in the food, and when they are drinking, the drink passes as if through a strainer.

They are not a foe anyone would have wanted to lose to. 'They embalm in cedar-oil the heads of the most distinguished of their enemies and keep them carefully in a chest: they display them with pride to strangers.'

Further reports from the time add to the image of the Celts and Gauls being altogether vicious. They are described as crazed warriors, running naked into battle. They are fond of drink. They string their enemies' heads around the necks of their horses. According to one source, they would even fight each other to the death for a decent bit of meat.

That was just the men. Their wives were every bit as tough. Diodorus said that they were the equals of their men in stature and courage, but later, in the fourth century, a Roman author, Ammianus Marcellinus, took that reputation and hammered it up a bit.

> A whole band of foreigners will be unable to cope with one of them in a fight, if he calls in his wife, stronger than he by far and with flashing eyes; least of all when she swells her neck and gnashes her teeth, and poising her huge white arms, begins to rain blows mingled with kicks, like shots discharged by the twisted cords of a catapult.

All of this is useful and amusing, but historians warn us that the Romans were liable to exaggerate their enemies' reputations, seeing that there was no point in claiming a magnificent victory if they hadn't first established the fearsome nature of the defeated enemy. They could even find a sort of nobility in the savages they encountered on their march westward. The most famous example of this is a sculpture, 'the Dying Gaul', which has survived as a copy of what was presumed to be an original third-century BC work. It depicts a Gallic warrior, naked except for a torc around his neck, and is a portrayal of the supposed dignity existing even in a barbarian.

Would the Gauls really have fought naked? Curiously, despite it sounding like a distinctly foolhardy tactic, it was described by several historians of the era, who often went out of their way to admire the physique of their enemy. The Gauls are thought likely to have been taller than the Romans, although most of the people the Romans came up against seem to have been taller than them, something which they were rather tetchy about. There was a minimum height requirement for the Roman army, but for rank and file legionnaires it may have been as low as 165 cm (5 ft 5 in.), so when they got up close to their enemies, they would have been fully aware of their inadequacies.

None of which fascinating detail leaves us much clearer about whether the Celts ever existed in the way that we later presumed they had. However, the Celts, whether or not it was in the guise of the Gauls, were mentioned enough for us to take notice, even if there is confusion or vagueness over where they lived and who exactly they were.

It's unhelpful that many of the surviving sources are themselves based on much earlier lost accounts, and that the whole lot has survived the couple of thousand years since in fragments only. For instance, an early reference to Ireland is believed to have come from a long-vanished sailing manual from about 600 BC, but which was used as a source almost a thousand years later by a fourth-century Latin poet, Rufus Festus Avienus. That poem is 'Ora Maritima' (Sea Coasts), and if its historical accuracy is ropey (Avienus never visited any of the places mentioned) it's not nearly as ropey as its artistic merit. With over 700 lines, it reads like the most long-winded set of directions anyone has ever received.

Still, it has proven worthwhile as a historical fragment, because the sailing manual Avienus quotes from gives some detail of the ancient Atlantic routes and the tin-producing regions and, along the way, he mentions that beyond the Oestrymnides islands was the land of the Celts, and they had taken it from the Ligurians. There are some problems here. First, we don't know where the Oestrymnides are, although they may be the islands off Brittany, or south of England. Second, the Ligurians were an Italian tribe that may have wandered all the way to the North Sea.

However, wherever the Oestrymnides are, Ireland is described as being north of them:

From here it is a two-day voyage to the Sacred Isle,
for by this name the ancients called the island.
It lies rich in turf among the waves,
thickly populated by the Hierni.
Nearby lies the island of the Albiones.

The *Hierni* are presumed to have been the Irish, and if the description was indeed based on an ancient sailing manual, then this counts as Ireland's debut in written history.

Roman and Greek accounts later adopted the term 'Hibernian', which is still familiar to us. It has been suggested that the Irish may have referred to their own island as *Iweriu*, a descendant of an Indo-European word meaning fat or fertile. This later became Eirú in Old Irish before evolving into Éire of today. Whether or not this is true, this word is used far more commonly in Britain than in Ireland, with the Irish having a certain aversion to it partly because of their neighbour's use of it, despite it being the word printed on every stamp sent out of the country.

Among other early references to Ireland are those of a Greek astronomer, Pytheas, from some time before 300 BC. While anything actually written in his hand is long gone, from subsequent accounts of his work we know that he took a journey north and became the first person to describe the Northern Lights, the midnight sun and the polar ice. He determined the true position of the pole star. He landed in Britain and not only noted the position of Ireland and described the Scandinavian sailors who journeyed there, but also named the island, calling it *Ierne*. Unfortunately, Pytheas didn't land on the island, so that's as much as we know about Ireland 300 years before Christ.

The very first map of Ireland was drawn by a Roman, Claudius Ptolemy, in about AD 150, although it was based on an earlier, lost work, of a fellow called Marinus of Tyre. His north-east coast is stretched towards Scotland, which is understandable given that Ireland would have been viewed from there but it was reasonably accurate nonetheless. The rivers are named. Only the west remains a bit vague.

Most notably, Ptolemy's map contains a list of 16 tribes, none of whom have what we would consider to be typically Irish names. This is sometimes treated as an intriguing clue as to when the Irish language actually took hold here. It has been argued, though, that it's simply because information about the island might have come from British sailors who wouldn't have been familiar with the local language anyway.

Ptolemy drew his map because, by then, the Roman Empire was touching on Ireland. After a few goes at it, the Romans finally conquered Britain from AD 43 and didn't leave for almost 400 years. There are a couple of things about this that are worth noting. First, we can be more certain that they landed in Ireland than the Celts ever did. And second, if Ireland was indeed Celtic, the Romans—a literate people obsessed with writing accounts of their various campaigns—never once thought to mention it.

———

From an Irish perspective it's easy to overlook how the Roman Empire was right on our doorstep. It has led to a great deal of speculation and controversy about whether they ever crossed the threshold.

There have been occasional outbreaks of media excitement, such as in 1996, when the *Sunday Times* announced: 'Fort discovery proves Romans invaded Ireland'.

It explained that,

A nondescript patch of land 15 miles north of Dublin has shattered one of Ireland's strongest myths. It indicates that the country was, after all, invaded by the Romans. For centuries its people believed it never happened. While Britain bent to the Roman yoke, the Irish were held to have lived in an heroic Celtic twilight on the fringes of the empire.

The *Sunday Times* accompanied the piece with an editorial that commented: 'Two fundamental axioms about Ireland that every schoolchild once learnt were that Ireland was free (a) from snakes and (b) from Romans. Both axioms now appear to be wild Irish bull.'

Reading this over their breakfast tables, Irish readers may have raised an eyebrow. When they reached the final line, they would have been forgiven for spluttering their cereal across the table. 'It was always obvious,' concluded the *Sunday Times*, 'that under the skin they were brothers as well as rivals of the other British.'

An invasion of Ireland by the Romans? Not quite. The site at Drumanagh, north Co. Dublin has never been officially excavated, and a handful of artefacts that come from it are stored in the National Museum of Ireland, their provenance yet to be revealed to the public or academia. In the interim, it has been subject to unseemly arguments, legal battles and even claims that there is a conspiracy of silence over Ireland's Roman past.

In many respects, of course, the myth of the heroic Celtic twilight has been shattered in recent years, but it wasn't the site at Drumanagh that did it. And the exact extent of Roman influence in Ireland at the time has indeed caused contention, but it has been a long time since anyone claimed that the island was free of their influence. They may not have invaded, but no one doubts that they were certainly here.

Ireland had something of a mixed reputation among Romans at the time. One writer, Strabo, has left an oft-quoted view of Ireland at the time of Christ as being a truly miserable place at the top of the world. It was 'home of men who are complete savages and lead a miserable existence because of the cold; and therefore, in my opinion, the northern limit of our inhabited world is to be placed there'.

Not wanting to ease up on the insults, Strabo really went for it, describing the occupants of Ireland as cannibalistic, inbred perverts. They were 'man-eaters as well as heavy eaters' who counted 'it an honourable thing, when their fathers die, to devour them, and openly to have intercourse, not only with other women, but also with their mothers and sisters'.

Pluckily, Strabo still wondered if the Romans should invade and take Ireland while they were in this part of the world. Ultimately, though, he was against the idea of the Romans even invading Britain, arguing that the cost of having a standing army there would be prohibitive. In this, he proved himself a better military strategist than travel guide. Within 50 years of his writing this, the Romans had finally taken Britain at their third attempt. They were to stay for almost 400 years, during which time they would be constantly overstretched.

Still, it seems that the Romans did consider the possibility of invading Ireland. Agricola, the Governor of Britain, is said to have remarked that 'one legion and a moderate number of auxiliaries' was all that would be needed to get the job done. Agricola, apparently, even brought an exiled king into his service in case an invasion of Ireland was launched. There is a teasing reference in the work of the Roman poet Juvenal, who later wrote that 'we have taken our arms beyond the shores of Ireland and the recently conquered Orkneys, and Britain of the short nights', but that is not backed up by any other contemporary accounts.

If the Romans ever did cross over in legions, the evidence has long since disappeared. Still, if they didn't come here as an invading force, Ireland would have been host to them as traders and sailors, as well as a haven to refugees fleeing their rule. There is plenty of evidence that the Romans (or at least the Roman British) visited, or that the Irish visited them. Among the bronze Roman brooches discovered in Ireland, a couple have been found in Newgrange, along with a torc inscribed with Roman letters. It's a reminder that even a couple of thousand years ago people were visiting the tomb as either pilgrims or just tourists.

Hoards of silver coins have turned up occasionally—1,700 of them in one Co. Derry spot—and they may be spoils from the looting of Roman Britain by the Irish. Or it's possible that coins may have been payment to Irish mercenaries who would have fought alongside the Romans during their British campaigns.

There are bodies too. At Lambay Island, off Rush (and close to the contentious land at Drumanagh), Roman-era graves and artefacts have been found. The dead may have been refugees from Britain, fleeing a revolt by the Brigante tribe. At Bray Head, Co. Wicklow there was a burial of some people who may have been traders, colonists, refugees or passing sailors. In their mouths were Roman coins, as was common when burying Roman dead—they were to pay the ferryman to take them across the River Styx to Hades. The stone cists in which the bodies lay were found in 1835, but they were subsequently destroyed and join the long list of historical finds that were lost soon after they were discovered.

In Stoneyford, Co. Kilkenny, close to the River Nore and upriver of the major port of Waterford, archaeologists have found the most obviously Roman burial site on the island, where the discovery of a female body indicates that there was once a permanent settlement, probably in the second century.

And what did the Irish give the Romans? Well, we know that they gave them at least one pack of big dogs thanks to a Roman who, in the late fourth century, wrote to his brother and told him about the 'seven Irish dogs' which 'so astonished Rome that it was thought they must have been brought in iron cages'. The dogs would have been used in the Roman games.

Ultimately, though, it seems that the Irish had a bigger military impact on the Romans than they had on us. In AD 367 Irish joined Picts of Scotland and Saxons of Germany in launching a massive, three-pronged attack on Britain's Romans. As the Roman strength weakened until finally being extinguished in the fifth century, the Irish turned coloniser, moving into various parts of Britain. Long before the British invaded Ireland, the traffic was in the other direction.

If the Roman evidence isn't enough to suggest that they came to Ireland as conquerors, it does confirm that they were not strangers to the island. And we know that the Irish would have adopted many of their customs and habits, not the least of them being Christianity.

It also throws something else into sharp focus. We can be more certain that they were here than the Celts ever were. Because you might think that, of any country, Ireland's ground should be practically stuffed with Celtic artefacts. In fact, the most striking thing is that there are hardly any at all.

———

The Hallstatt period, as named after those finds at the salt mountain in western Austria, came to be divided into four segments, according to their technologies and the way in which they buried their dead. They are rather baldly categorised as Hallstatt A, Hallstatt B, Hallstatt C and Hallstatt D. However, the first two are described as 'proto-Celtic' and only the latter two as 'Celtic'.

Putting it at its most simple, Hallstatt A lasted from 1200 to 1000 BC and was a sophisticated Bronze Age culture, during which salt mines were dug as deep as a couple of hundred metres, with shafts as wide as 17 m. The people cremated their dead and placed the ashes in urns, meaning that this is often described as an urnfield culture. This contrasts with Hallstatt B, which lasted a couple of centuries or so and during which people were some-times buried under raised mounds.

Moving into the short-lived Hallstatt C (800–700 BC), which covered the early part of the Iron Age, the rich were buried with their goods—including, for those who could afford it, four-wheeled chariots. Finally, in Hallstatt D—also so short it may have lasted only three or four generations until about 480 BC—we find luxury Mediterranean goods in graves, the influence of the Greeks having spread northwards and westwards.

There's a reason why that chronology is worth spelling out, and it's because there is no Hallstatt E. Instead, the Celtic chronology segues into La Tène, based on the Swiss discovery of 2,000 artefacts. The La Tène period gives us the first coherent notion of a warrior culture, of feasts and drinking, of geometric patterns in art. Again, it reflects the growing influence of the Greeks on the region, with trade centres shifting as a result. The rich were now buried with two-wheeled chariots and warriors were buried in a way that emphasised their military prowess.

The Hallstatt finds can be linked with finds from across the Continent, sweeping an area from northern France to the west to Slovenia in the east. La Tène finds extend farther, taking in much of the Continent. It becomes clear that among the problems of linking La Tène culture with the Celts is that they were not a neat tribe, concentrated in a single area. Instead, they were spread across Europe. There were regional variations, and influences from elsewhere. For example, from the first century BC onwards, the influence of the expanding Roman Empire begins to mutate the culture, most obviously regarding religious beliefs.

There are commonalities across the region, and one of them was in the art. That Celtic style we are so familiar with now developed during this time. What archaeologists ask, though, is if a cultural unifier should be confused with ethnic unification. Just because there was a recognisable 'Celtic' art, should it mean that we presume every tribe that adopted it was Celtic?

The Celts were, then, almost everywhere in central Europe at this time, but it is clear to historians that this array of tribes would not have considered themselves part of one great Celtic family. While elements of language, culture and tools were shared across the region, they did not form a unified, organised group. These Celtic peoples, as we might like to see them, were unlikely to have been one people at all but separate tribes, occasionally coalescing, sharing culture with trade and warfare.

The evidence of that shared culture focuses on northern central Europe and moves outwards, with finds scattered in each direction. But where Hallstatt and La Tène sites are plentiful in the heartland, they become increasingly rare the farther west you go. There are some rich sites in northern France, but Hallstatt culture seems to have only brushed Britain and by the time you get to Ireland they cease almost entirely. And the culture of La Tène, that period considered the most Celtic, has left numerous objects in southern Britain but not all that many in Ireland. This was considered to be one of the great cultural shifts in European history; a period when the Celts were supposed to have spread far and wide. If you knew nothing about Ireland's proclaimed Celtic identity, you would guess that Ireland was one of the least Celtic lands there is.

If you want Celtic artefacts, go to France. They've plenty: Celtic brooches, Celtic pottery, Celtic swords, Celtic chariots. That's where the bodies are buried, literally. In Ireland, not a single typically Celtic grave has been found, which compares badly with the three sites on the east coast that have been identified as Roman burials. There isn't a chariot or even a shard of pottery from the culture. The number of decorated brooches from the period remains in only single figures. From the time when the Celts were supposed to have arrived in Ireland the cupboard is not overflowing.

It has been guessed that the Iron Age reached Ireland at about 300 BC, when the population switched—as was the case elsewhere—from using bronze. How the technology involved in creating iron arrived here is not known. It may have been through small groups of immigrants; it may have been learned by the Irish abroad. Either way, we don't have many clues to go by.

From the Hallstatt era, we have slim pickings, with most finds appearing around rivers and suggesting that the iron objects, and some of their influence, had been imported, but not that many of its people were. Obviously, Ireland's museums would be much richer—and our understanding clearer—if so much of the island's historical evidence hadn't been mishandled, lost, damaged or pilfered.

It was not a problem confined to that era. Ireland has quite stringent laws on who can and who cannot carry out archaeological searches, and the reason why they are needed is clear. The National Museum of Ireland has made particular efforts to find stolen goods. During the late 1980s, for instance, it recovered thousands of items, finding them as far away as Australia. At the time, the museum claimed that, in terms of profitability, the trade in stolen antiquities was second only to the international drugs trade.

Sometimes they didn't have to look too hard to find the booty. In 1991, an Irishman, Peter Kenny, rang Boston College with the offer of fifth- and sixth-century gravestones he claimed had been looted by his distant ancestors and had been in the family ever since. They had, in fact, been stolen from St Dermot's monastic site on Inchcleraun Island, Co. Longford. Kenny then sailed to Miami with the stone slabs, a Viking anchor, several coins and a selection of antique guns. He might have got away with it too, if it wasn't for a ham radio enthusiast who overheard a conversation involving Irish Republican fundraising, Australian bank accounts and land deals.

Kenny had arranged to meet with a Boston College professor. What he didn't realise was that from the moment he arrived, almost everyone he met—including the students and staff who helped him lift the gravestones into the university building—were undercover FBI agents. Nor did he realise that a 'wealthy benefactor' the professor had introduced him to was a wired agent.

Having shaken hands on what he must have thought was a very sweet deal, Kenny left the College, returned to his motel and got something of a surprise when the FBI appeared and arrested him. He spent four months in a US jail before being deported to Ireland, convicted and imprisoned for 12 months. The antiquities theft ring he worked with was broken up as a result.

In the nineteenth century, the penalties for looting were nonexistent but the opportunities great. In 1854, for instance, while building the Limerick to Ennis line, railway workers unearthed a staggering gold hoard, with hundreds of pieces of jewellery. This is called the Great Clare Find, traced to the Iron Age, but we will never know exactly how great it was because once it was dug up it triggered a scramble during which much of it was either sold for small sums or melted down. Contemporary records tell us of about 150 gold items. Only 26 survive, split between the National Museum of Ireland and the British Museum. 'It was by far the greatest find of associated gold objects found in Western Europe,' sighed the archaeologist Robert Macalister in 1921, 'and the loss to science of the great bulk is most deplorable.'

There was also an excited plundering of a site at Lisnacrogher, Co. Antrim after it began to reveal its hoard during the second half of the 1800s. Peat cutters found evidence that this was an Iron Age settlement of some importance, although the accounts left behind from the time express ignorance as to what exactly it was. There was a building housing some sort of metalwork facility, but even now we don't know what its precise function was. As for the rest of the area, it was fleeced by collectors and the site was virtually destroyed.

Still, about 80 objects from the Lisnacrogher site remain, enough to confirm it as the greatest bounty of La Tène artefacts ever found in Ireland. The scabbards and swords had been made there using iron mined nearby. It seems that whoever made them was doing so with deep knowledge—perhaps passed on through generations—of the style.

What makes Lisnacrogher particularly interesting, though, is that there has been nothing else of its scale found anywhere in Ireland. No other archaeological discovery has yet been found that comes close to matching it. In fact, the south and south-west of the island has revealed virtually nothing from the La Tène period. This suggests that the region around Lisnacrogher, the north-east of Ireland, was the place where either a small number of people arrived, or from where the Irish picked up continental influences and returned with them. Perhaps the impact of that culture was limited to small numbers of immigrants, or that the objects arrived as gifts, purchases or that the traders and sailors of that part of Ireland were most likely to spot these developments in northern Britain and bring the ideas home with them.

There are other notable finds, such as four La Tène trumpets that turned up under water at Loughnashade, Co. Armagh—only one of which survives now. It looks very like the trumpet that is at the feet of the sculpture of the dying Gaul.

Relatively few weapons have been found, with only a couple of dozen La Tène swords, and eight scabbards, in the whole country. But the Celtic influence on these is offset by how short they are compared with the long slashing swords used by the Celts in Europe. Only one complete shield has been discovered, in a Tipperary bog. Like the swords, it is small compared with the European finds, because Irish combat tended to be at close quarters, with short weapons used to stab at the enemy. Scars across the Tipperary shield give tantalising proof that it had been used in at least one fight.

There is no surprise that bows haven't been found in Ireland, because they weren't used during the La Tène period. Slings, however, were used but none of them have been found either.

A few finds, such as an oak road across a Co. Longford bog that has been precisely dated to 148 BC, confirm that wheeled transport was used on the country's routes back then. However, we've yet to dig up any of the war chariots found elsewhere and which are depicted on Celtic coins. And unlike some of their European counterparts, those Irish rich enough to afford wheeled transport didn't find room for it in their graves.

The lack of goods means that we have few ideas of everyday life during the Iron Age. A tankard found in Antrim may have been used for beer; bone dice hint at the games played; the jewellery that's been discovered has included anklets, beads, finger and toe rings, and possibly a pair of earrings, as well as rings that must once have belonged to belts. A couple of mirrors have been found and a pair of tweezers. There is a pair of shears for cutting hair and bone combs for brushing it. There is, however, no Iron Age settlement to give us an idea of the kind of house in which their owners would have done their personal grooming.

Occasionally, though, something truly wonderful has been unearthed. A twisted gold torc found in Co. Roscommon dates from the third century BC and seems to be of La Tène influence, as does another torc found alongside it from the same period. The first may have been made in Ireland, but the latter is likely to have come from the Rhineland. We can't be sure that it wasn't brought here as a gift, a bribe or a purchase. That both were placed in a bog has led archaeologists to speculate that they may have been left there as a spiritual offering.

A wonderful hoard of gold found at Broighter, Co. Derry in 1896 included a delicate gold boat, now on display in the National Museum of Ireland. It's more than just a pretty ornament, because this is the closest thing we have to a boat from this era of Irish history. Archaeologists have gleaned a surprising amount from it, including that a life-sized version would have had room for about 18 oarsmen, and there still would have been space for provisions and even passengers.

Gold is rare from this time, so such finds are not only treasured, but also intriguing. We can only guess at how they ended up being left where they were. They may have been loot, stolen and stored but not returned for, or they may have been religious offerings. Either way, you can't help but wonder what predicament a person would have to have been in to abandon such treasures, or to trust that something so precious would placate or flatter the gods.

In Ireland, even the art that popular culture considers the very epitome of Celtic developed separately from that in Europe. After an initial flourishing of the art we associate with the Celts— patterns based on tendrils and leaves—a more conservative style soon took over, in which the artists proved unwilling to experiment or deviate from the prescribed style. From the turn of the first millennium on, it has more in common with British rather than continental art, proving that people were travelling back and forth across the Irish Sea during this time. Even then, it is still considered to have become recognisably Irish.

It may be that there is much more still hidden out there, just waiting to be found, although as the Irish peatlands are cut away there are diminishing opportunities for a surprise. It's certain that the great amounts that have been plundered over the centuries have robbed us of a fuller understanding of the time. It is far more likely, though, that there is a paucity of evidence because little exists here. It is on this hard truth that the idea of a mass migration of Celts to Ireland has foundered.

What has instead emerged is evidence of a gradual Celtic influence, concentrated in pockets. It seems that any people who came here from areas influenced by the Hallstatt or La Tène cultures were a minority, encountering a population that had already developed a sophisticated civilisation during the Stone and Bronze Ages. Newgrange was already 3,000 years old by the time the Celtic people were supposed to have migrated to Ireland.

There was certainly an influence from the La Tène peoples, but it has been argued that throughout this period Ireland was being influenced by a number of regions: Iberia, Britain, Rome, the Rhineland, the eastern Mediterranean and Gaul. It has been pointed out that it is not a simple historical equation in which Bronze Age equals pre-Celtic and Iron Age equals Celtic. In fact, according to the archaeologist Barry Raftery, there is a straightforward continuity between those very first people who came here 10,000 years ago until the fifth century, when Celtic societies were supposed to have flourished across Europe. Raftery was the professor of Celtic Archaeology at University College Dublin, so he's worth listening to.

And yet, there has always been the small matter of the languages spoken to varying degrees in the regions that consider themselves to be Celtic. There are now many historians, though, who wouldn't see the Celtic culture as being anything other than a linguistic one. Whether that is an excuse to define the Irish as Celtic is not readily accepted. One leading Welsh linguist, D. Ellis Evans, has warned that this is an area in which to tread cautiously, recommending, in fact, that we be 'ruthlessly restrained'.

In the Middle Ages, there was no such uncertainty. The source of the Irish language had been precisely traced to the tower of Babel. It was believed that Fénius Farsaid—a King of Sythia in the Middle East, and ancestor of the Gaels—travelled to the tower with 72 scholars (one to study each of the languages created there). However, they got there to find that the tribes had already been scattered, so Fénius dispatched his scholars to study each tongue, while he stayed at the tower and co-ordinated the operation from there.

Ten years later, the scholars returned from their missions and asked Fénius to create a language out of the confusion of tongues, a language that would be theirs alone. The result was Gaelic. Any Irish person who has ever used a smattering of the language when trying to surreptitiously gossip abroad will know that, in a way, it had a successful outcome.

Obviously, the reality is probably somewhat less grand, and even less certain. The origins of the language remain distant and unknown. It may once have seemed natural to assume that it arrived on the boats that brought the Celtic masses to Ireland, but without such an invasion there are awkward questions about how the so-called Celtic languages reached the western isles of Europe, and even just how Celtic they actually are.

In the modern world, we have come to understand the Celtic languages as being those spoken chiefly along the north Atlantic seaboard, in Ireland, Wales, Scotland, the Isle of Man, Cornwall and Brittany, yet the evidence seems to suggest that the original elements of a Celtic language were spoken as far away as Asia Minor, as well as in the Iberian peninsula, in Italy and along the Danube. It is seen as an early offshoot of the Indo-European language which is considered to have been the earliest language on the Continent, but the evidence for this is incomplete, meaning that it is a theoretical tongue.

Still, there is uncertainty over whether there was a single proto-Celtic language from which all others emerged, or whether they were separate languages from the very beginning. It has even been suggested by one scholar that Irish—or the strand which it is cat-egorised under—was the first to break away from proto-Celtic.

Whatever the background to such a proto-Celtic language, aca-demics have divided the Celtic languages into four families. Once again, Edward Lhuyd has his fingerprints all over this theory.

It was he who first came up with the observation that there are the Continental and Insular strands of the Celtic languages, although these are largely geographical distinctions, used, as the historian Barry Cunliffe has pointed out, 'for convenience'.

The Insular languages are those of Ireland and the British Isles. Continental Celtic, as the name reveals, is the language once spoken on the Continent, but which is now extinct. The exception to this is the language of Brittany, which was settled by Britons around the third century, who brought their Insular language with them. It has long been presumed that Celtic was the language spoken in Britain before the arrival of the Romans, who were later followed by the Angle tribe of Germany, who gave the world the English language. It is thought that those Britons who were pushed out and into Brittany either brought their language with them, or possibly reinforced the Gaulish language already spoken there.

Anyway, the other linguistic distinction is made between the Celtic languages spoken in Ireland, Scotland and the Isle of Man, and those spoken in Wales, Cornwall and Brittany. Welsh and Irish speakers know that to be fluent in one is of no advantage in becoming even passable in the other. They sound, and read, utterly different. They are described as being either Goidelic or Brythonic, or alternatively as Q Celtic and P Celtic, which at its most basic means that they are defined depending on how each pronounces the qu- sound. It is a k- in Irish, but in Welsh is often softened to a p-. For instance, in Irish the number four is *ceithir*, but in Welsh it is *pedwar*. Again, there are some modern doubts over whether even this detail is significant enough to warrant such focus.

The Irish language is thought to be the more archaic of the two strands of Insular Celtic, and both Scottish and Manx are considered offshoots of Old Irish. The Irish probably introduced Gaelic to Scotland, where it seems that the language supplanted a previous language spoken by the Picts.

Its origins, though, are lost. Did Irish emerge from western Europe, or was it picked up through the busy trade routes of the Atlantic seaboard? Is Irish even a Celtic language, or a mix of Celtic and another language or languages already native to the island? Or is it an amalgam of several Celtic languages, a localised version of Celtic or a bit of both?

Tracing its origins is not helped by the lack of written history. The first evidence of language in Ireland comes from the Ogham scripts, which were inscribed on stones, and based mainly on intersecting lines, although vowels are occasionally represented by dots along a vertical line. They are considered to have been written in Old Irish, and yet they are based on the Latin alphabet, so we presume they developed during the 400 or so years that the Romans were in Britain. A date of about AD 300 has been settled on, because it gives enough time for Latin schools to have become established in Britain.

Ogham can be found carved into about 400 stones that stretch in a rough arc from Kerry across to Wales, and at a number of points above and below it from southern Scotland to Cornwall. It is assumed that it was brought to Britain by Irish migrants.

Most of the stones have a name scratched on them, letting others know either who owned it or the land on which it was placed. Where exactly the inscriptions originated from remains a mystery, but the Ogham stones at least give a starting point from which we can trace the evolution of the Irish language. It means that we can identify its position at a certain point along its journey, if not where it came from.

———

It becomes clear why all of this uncertainty and doubt has caused more than a modicum of angst among academics who have specialised in the various aspects of Celtic studies. In 1996 an English professor of Celtic Studies, Patrick Sims-Williams, wrote an essay in which he succinctly outlined the crisis of identity gripping the subject. 'A number of us in or around the discipline of Celtic Studies have already been starting to question its historical basis, validity and identity,' he explained. He then listed some of the problems:

> . . . ancient and medieval writers never used the term Celtic to describe the peoples and languages of Britain and Ireland; the medieval Irish and Welsh did not believe that they sprang from a common stock and showed no fraternal feelings for each other; the vernacular literature of Wales and Ireland seem to have been less open to mutual influence than to influences from Latin, French and English; the Irish and Welsh hardly seem to have perceived the special affinities between their languages before Edward Lhuyd (1707); and the idea of 'Celtic literature' hardly existed before Ernst Renan (1854). Even today it is arguable whether many Celtic speakers regard themselves as having a 'Celtic' ethnic identity over and above their undoubted Welsh, Breton, Irish or Scottish identity—any more than

English-speakers and Icelandic-speakers think of themselves as having a 'Teutonic' identity.

Again, these were only *some* of the problems.

Sims-Williams admitted that, 'Such doubts oblige modern Celticists to reconsider the validity of the parameters of their discipline and to take it apart—albeit in the hope of putting it back together in a more convincing way.'

The crisis was understandable given that, in a relatively short space of time, the Celts had gone from being a race and culture that had seeded some of our modern nations to a disappeared people, whose very existence, some believed, was based on more wishful thinking than evidence.

Sims-Williams' epiphany was far from being the moment at which the idea of the Celtic civilisation collapsed entirely, but was a neat summary of how much attitudes towards it had changed. The edifice had already been cracked by the publication of a couple of essays in a 1983 collection, *The Invention of Tradition*, which looked at how certain cultural traditions were actually modern creations, invented or adapted to suit an ideological purpose.

Then, a 1992 book by Malcolm Chapman, *The Celts: The Construction of a Myth*, rigorously examined and undercut assumptions that a common language meant a common heritage. By the time Simon James's *The Atlantic Celts* was published in 1999, arguing that the identity of the so-called Celtic nations was formed around ideas of a common language and fanned by cultural nationalism, the wider media began to pay attention. But even as the newspapers revelled in this supposedly iconoclastic story, academic orthodoxy had, in fact, already switched.

It was already clear that while elements of language, culture and tools were shared across the region, it did not mean that they formed a unified, organised group; that even though there were certain connections between the people of continental Europe, this didn't necessarily extend to Ireland; and that the remnants of the Celts, in whatever form they existed, are on mainland Europe, not its western fringe.

A couple of years after his original bout of angst, Patrick Sims-Williams returned to the problems facing Celtic studies in an essay, 'Celtomania and Celtoscepticism'. During the intervening period, he had found an accommodation of sorts between the aims of his discipline and the uncomfortable facts it had been built upon. Celtic studies had a future, he wrote, because, regardless of the evidence—or lack of it—for the Celts, a collective identity had since developed for the people of Scotland, Wales, Ireland, Brittany, the Isle of Man and Cornwall. It may be a construction, but it was still legitimate to study it.

Yet, a twist was just around the corner. It was about to be shown that there was a link between the Celtic regions that went beyond language or culture or a collective sense of identity; that there was an ancient connection between the Basques, Galicians, Bretons, Cornish, Manx, Irish, Welsh and Scottish that was several thousand years old at least. It turned out that these people had been carrying the clues inside them all along—it was only now that science had figured out how to unlock the genetic code.

At the Smurfit Institute of Genetics, a relatively anonymous building in a corner of Trinity College Dublin, they have spent some years working on the many pieces that go towards answering one simple question: where did the Irish come from? The geneticists do not have all the answers. It is not simply a case of digging up a body, scraping off a bit of DNA and throwing it under a microscope. For a start, even if a decent Mesolithic body was found, the site would need to be sealed off and treated like a crime scene to have any hope of keeping the body relatively clean. As it is, old bones tend to carry very little DNA but do accumulate a lot of fungus, moss and dirt. If you just licked your finger before turning the page, you've probably left more DNA behind on this book than would be on an ancient bone.

Even then, it would be hard to tell whether it was the correct DNA.

When one ancient tooth was found in Greenland, the geneticists who studied it had reason to hope that it would provide genetic information. A tooth is considered to be a useful fragment, and the cold would have been a great preservative. So they tested it, only to find that it carried the DNA of 14 different people.

There has been some progress in this field, with a technique developed through which scientists look at bones to get a history of their owner and whether he came from the place where he was found or if he had migrated from somewhere else.

The oldest Irish body yet to have its DNA extracted is that of a child, between two and four years of age, who was placed in a cave in the Burren during the Bronze Age, some 3,500 years ago. It was among the remains of eight people, including a newborn baby, and animal bones.

The child's lower leg bone was sent to a laboratory in Mainz, Germany, where the DNA was analysed. From that, it was found that the child's genetic family had originated in northern Europe about 50,000 years ago.

It was a precious discovery because this kind of opportunity is rare in Ireland, where many of the bones that have been found were charred from cremation, and the Irish soil is unkind to those that weren't. So geneticists have instead looked to the DNA of modern people for clues as to where their ancestors might have come from. And they've discovered that the Irish share what is described as a 'non-random affinity' with the other peoples of the Atlantic coast of Europe. Quite what this means isn't certain, but Trinity's Brian McEvoy, from the team that carried out the research, guesses that it's probably a link that leads us back at least to the first farmers, because when they began to farm, humans stayed in one spot, lived in larger groups and gradually became more difficult to shift. Those genetic markers would have become rooted with them.

It may be that the bloodline goes back further, because if, as some have speculated, the language of the Basque country is something so different that it may in fact be a remnant of the language spoken in that part of Europe before the arrival of the Indo-European tongues, then it may be that a genetic link between the Irish and that region could go all the way back to the first people. This, though, is conjecture.

What does all of that have to do with the Celts? In a way, it's just another blow to the already battered idea that a Celtic race swept in from central Europe and to the western fringes of the Continent. If that had happened, then the Irish DNA would have a lot more in common with the people of Switzerland.

Instead, the Irish find their cousins along the Atlantic façade. Yet, while this does nothing to resuscitate the Celts, at the very least it tells us that the story of those people who now believe themselves to be Celts, to believe themselves to have a shared heritage that bonds them today, is, after all, an ancient one. There may be no Celtic nations, but their people still have something special in common.

Chapter 3 ~

HIT AND RUN AND SETTLE DOWN: THE VIKINGS

The Vikings took over a corner of Europe, moved around in large numbers, announced themselves in spectacular fashion and were good enough to write some of it down. It means that we know a fair amount about them. So let's start with something most of us have always presumed was true: the Vikings wore horned helmets.

They never did. Not once. It makes a lot of sense once you think about it for even a few seconds. In close combat, horns would only have given an opponent something to grab on to. They would have been difficult to stack and, if you had them lying around on a ship, they would have punctured any backside that sat on one. In short, horned headgear would have been pretty much useless for any purpose.

A few horned helmets have turned up across Europe, dating as far back as the Bronze Age, but they are believed to have been ceremonial dress rather than battle gear and, anyway, none of them relate to the Viking era. Even then, they are not the ox-horned helmets we're so familiar with, but have twisted horns.

The stereotype of the horned helmet gained ground through the nineteenth century, mostly thanks to the imagination of the costume designer working on the original production of Richard Wagner's *Ring Cycle* in 1876. The opera's story included nothing whatsoever to do with Vikings, but it did feature Valkyries of Norse myth, and the costume designer received some confused inspiration for their headgear from a tour of Scandinavian museums. Vikings, by the way, never wore winged helmets either, which was an image given to them by the Romantics of the seventeenth and eighteenth centuries. The fictional Valkyries, as it happens, did.

An avalanche of cultural confusion has since contributed to the horned helmet becoming the Vikings' signature feature, from Hagar the Horrible to the tourists on Dublin's Viking Splash tours who cheer through the streets on an amphibious boat while holding on to their plastic horns. It would be churlish, and a little childish, to yell back at them something about how they are only perpetuating a myth based on historical misinterpretation and popular ignorance.

What did the Vikings wear on their heads? A lot of them wore nothing, and those who did probably wore leather, conical headgear. Although, one German discovery revealed a helmet with a visor and chain mail to protect the neck. It is an attractive, intimidating piece of headgear, which could probably be afforded only by leading warriors. And it has no horns.

That somewhat disappointing revelation, of course, is hardly enough to jettison the stereotype of the Vikings as bloodthirsty, rampaging pillagers. As it happens, they *were* bloodthirsty, rampaging pillagers, but they were a good deal more than that. They were such effective entrepreneurs and diplomats that they created a sphere of influence that stretched from the Arctic circle to the north coast of Africa.

However, it would be unfair to remember the Vikings as nothing more than violent raiders. They were that, but when they came to Ireland they ended up bringing with them far more than mere terror. They brought culture, money, technology, people and towns. Within a short time of their arrival, they began to build Dublin, a town which they turned into one of the richest ports in western Europe. Over time, the Scandinavian raiders became colonisers. And eventually they became Irish.

Within not more than a century of first venturing out of Scandinavia, the Vikings had reached as far south as Spain, north Africa and Italy. They had attacked Hamburg. They had sacked Paris and then gone back to sack it again. They had spread east into Russia and gone west to colonise Iceland. They triggered a reshaping of the Church across western Europe and had a major impact on the power struggles across the region. They conquered much of Britain, and although they never had such control of Ireland, soon after arriving they had founded Dublin, established themselves in Cork, Waterford and Wexford, and had developed a thriving economy based on slavery, war, plunder and a great many offshoot industries. All of which was a decent achievement for a people who had spent the previous few hundred years huddled along the northern fringes of Europe staying out of harm's way.

What we know of the pre-Viking age comes from archaeological evidence only. Nothing was documented, so there is a certain amount of guesswork involved in explaining why exactly a previously insular race suddenly turned its ambitions outwards. They had been too far north to be conquered by the Romans, so that as much of Europe underwent upheaval as a result of the fall of Rome, the Vikings developed their own technology and society away from such influence. It ultimately meant that they would go on to replace the Romans as the great empire of north-western Europe.

At this time in history, before the late 700s when the Vikings began raiding Europe, Norway's coastal regions were habitable, but fenced off by imposing mountain ranges. Much of inland Sweden was densely forested and covered in bog interspersed by lakes, and it was close enough to the Jutland peninsula to establish economic ties with the Danes.

Living on these indented, island-dotted coastlines, where it was often easier to travel across water than land, it was natural that the Vikings would develop as a seagoing people. There is some debate over whether it was the urge to travel that encouraged boat-building, or it was better boat-building that triggered the Viking expansion—but whatever the reason, they gradually became perhaps the best boat builders on the planet.

There are examples of boats from AD 400 that are clearly earlier versions of the boats that would turn up in Ireland over four centuries later. But as the boats became more advanced, travel farther afield and more time on sea was possible. We don't know exactly what innovation first encouraged the Vikings' adventures, but they extended the size of the hull, deepened the keel and increased the size of the mast and sails they could carry. The manoeuvrability of the vessel became greater, the speeds faster.

Trading boats had rooms on board, the central one being given over to the freight, with a room for crew. But the boat that we have come to recognise as being quintessentially Viking—the longship—really did live up to its name. Capable of carrying 60 men or more, it had a hull shallow enough to be sailed close to shore, and dragged onto a beach. Being open, it was easy to get in or out of it, so very useful for raiding. The Vikings would spend about 300 years proving it.

The Vikings' pillaging was originally a localised affair. A combination of better boats and busier trade routes meant that piracy became such a problem that coastal areas of Scandinavia became depopulated as a result. Meanwhile, the borders within Norway and Sweden shifted regularly as chieftains vied for local supremacy. So, there was no centralised power under which the Viking fleets sailed. Instead, as growing population pressures coincided with improvements in marine technology, the first raiders went on freelance missions.

As they began to venture south from Scandinavia, the boats would have been crewed by part-time raiders, possibly under the leadership of the local aristocrat. These were men who would have farmed during the off-season, and then gathered together at the harbours as the weather improved, heading out to plunder. Setting out on their voyages, they would have hugged the coast, only

crossing the open sea at the shortest points and in the best conditions. They might have stopped to cook meals and to get fresh
water, and stayed ashore longer when taking shelter from storms.

The point at which they began to export themselves, the
acknowledged beginning of the Viking Age, is commonly dated as
beginning in 793. The first recorded raid outside of Scandinavia
occurred in this year at Lindisfarne, a tidal island off England's
east coast, and the chief description of it comes from the Anglo-
Saxon Chronicle. And what a description it is.

> This year came dreadful fore-warnings over the land of the
> Northumbrians, terrifying the people most woefully: these were
> immense sheets of light rushing through the air, and whirl-
> winds, and fiery, dragons flying across the firmament. These
> tremendous tokens were soon followed by a great famine: and
> not long after, on the sixth day before the ides of January in the
> same year, the harrowing inroads of heathen men made lamen-
> table havoc in the church of God in Holy-island, by rapine and
> slaughter.

There is no such bluster from the Irish annals. In fact, they give
such an underwhelming version of events that it has caused argument ever since. Our best guess is that the Vikings first arrived in
Ireland early on the morning of a decent summer's day in 795,
when they sailed quietly up the boomerang-shaped coastline of
Antrim's Rathlin Island and chose a spot to drag the boat ashore.
They would then have crept towards the island's monastery,
where monks who had chosen a peaceful, penitent life would have
found themselves treated to a rather nasty surprise. Having plundered what they could, the Vikings would then have pushed their
ship out to sea in the glow of a flaming monastery.

That's all conjecture, though, because the written record of this
raid is, to say the least, scant. Of this momentous day in Irish
history, the Annals of Ulster tells us only this:

The burning of Rechru by the pagans, and Skye was plundered and robbed.

That's it. One sentence, inserted among entries that are really just death notices of various important figures. If there's one thing historians have come to accept, it's that you look to the annals for bare facts only. And that even these will not always be completely transparent.

The Annals of Ulster, for example, were compiled in the fifteenth century but possibly sourced from a story known as far back as the seventh century.

Nor were its writers interested in always fleshing out the detail of events we now see as pivotal. The Annals of Ulster entry for 794, the year before the Vikings arrived in Ireland, mentions the 'devastation of all the islands of Britain by heathens' and nothing more. Even after the first Irish raid, the annals give a cursory mention to the Vikings' return in 798 when they plundered the monastery at Holmpatrick, Skerries, halfway down the east coast, stealing cattle and destroying its shrine. The annals are understandably more concerned with other events, such as a storm in 804 which killed 1,010 on an island off the Clare coastline. In all, though, the annals' ability to understate seismic events manages to be tantalising and often deeply frustrating.

As it happens, we can't even be clear on what that one sentence about the Vikings' first raid actually refers to. The 'Rechru' mentioned is generally believed to have been Rathlin, but there has long been speculation that it may have been Lambay Island, off Dublin's east coast, which also had the ancient name of Rechru and was certainly a target of later Viking raids. It is assumed that Rathlin was the Vikings' first stop chiefly because it was on their route as they travelled south from Norway, past Scotland, raiding Skye on the way. Although, even the reference to Skye has been questioned and may in fact have been saying simply that a 'shrine was plundered and robbed'. And the 'pagans' bit is often translated as 'heathens'. It's just one sentence, but with several possible meanings.

It is presumed that the 'pagans' are the Vikings, because none of the annals used the word 'Vikings' at any point. They were not called the Vikings in Britain either. Instead, a range of terms was used: they were *genti*, or 'heathens' or the *Gailli*, 'foreigners'. The Norse were *Finngaill* and the Danes *Dubhgaill*, but they could also be *Nordmainn* and *Nordmanni* ('Northmen').

In fact, the Vikings were hardly referred to as Vikings by anybody other than themselves. Even then, we don't know whether the term 'Viking'—*vikingr* in Old Norse—was adapted because *vik* is the word for inlet, and may have related to the people of the Vík district of the Oslo Fjord, or because 'to vike' was a verb for raiding and pillaging.

For some colour about the raiders—most of it blood red—we can turn to a twelfth-century text, *Cogadh Gaedhel re Gallaibh* (The Wars of the Irish with the Foreigners). Here we read about 'astonishing and awful great oppression over all Erinn, throughout its breadth, by powerful azure Norsemen, and by fierce hard-hearted Danes' that was brought upon 'every house' by these 'valiant, wrathful, foreign, purely pagan people'. During one Viking onslaught, its author explains, Ireland 'became filled with immense floods, and countless sea-vomitings of ships, and boats, and fleets'.

Apart from using the verb 'sea-vomitings' for probably the one and only time in written literature, the *Cogadh* had a great interest in portraying the Vikings as vicious because it had been commissioned as a glorification of Brian Boru and his dynasty. Written at the request of the descendants of Boru, it was an exceptionally successful piece of propaganda, exaggerating and lionising Boru's prowess to such an extent that it contributed greatly to the long-held idea that he was the man who, at the Battle of Clontarf in 1014, kicked the Vikings out of Ireland, although not before he was treacherously stabbed in his own tent.

Written a century after that battle, it was useful for it to enforce the idea of Ireland as being shaken by the savagery of the Vikings. It was not, it must be said, a baseless accusation. During the Vikings' early raids on Ireland their reputation was a fearsome one as revealed by a verse written in the margins of a manuscript, presumably by a monk who had either experienced or heard about the Vikings' tactics:

Fierce and wild is the wind tonight
Tossing the tresses of the sea to white
On such a night as this I feel at ease
Fierce Northmen only course the quiet seas

The arrival of raiders was dreaded, because the consequences could be so devastating that those island-dwelling monks were occasionally forced to move to the mainland as a result.

By 795, having plundered islands off the British coast, the Vikings introduced themselves to Ireland, not only at Rathlin Island but also off the west coast at the monasteries on Inishmurray and Inishbofin. It's reasonable to assume that the same raiders may have been responsible for all three attacks.

It did not lead to a great wave of pillaging, but a gradual prodding of the coastline, during which the Vikings year by year skirted the north coast and moved farther and farther south. There has to be a certain suspicion of the statistics given by the annals, because the monks who wrote them were likely to have more knowledge of the raids on monasteries, and a greater incentive to make a note of them. Nevertheless, for the first quarter of the ninth century, there was an average of one raid per year, although these would have come in clusters. Between 813 and 821 the annals make no mention of any Viking raids at all. In fact, in the first 25 years of the ninth century, 87 raids on monasteries are blamed on the Irish.

The monasteries had long been battlegrounds between rival clans and it is thought that monks would have engaged in combat when the situation required it. Some of their territories stretched across large areas, and they were wealthy enough that they often became the subject of political rivalries. Monasteries fought each other, fell victim to local feuds, or became allies on one side or the other. They affiliated with local kings and abbots fell in battle on occasion. For example, an Annals of Ulster entry for 807 tells us of 'a battle between the community of Corcach and the community of Cluain Ferta Brénainn, among whom resulted a slaughter of a countless number of ordinary ecclesiastics and of eminent men of the community of Corcach'. (This is the same year in which we are tantalised with news that the 'Moon was turned the colour of blood'.)

The monasteries of Clonmacnoise and Birr in Co. Offaly were at war in 760, with Clonmacnoise then going into battle against Durrow four years later. There were large battles at Ferns for half a century until 817, as kings attempted to gain control.

So, while the Vikings did wreak havoc on the monastic settlements, they were not the first to do it. It was a bloody time. The Annals of the Four Masters gives a sense of just how bloody through a sequence of entries for 807:

807.11: A slaughter was made of the foreigners by the men of Umhall.
807.12: A slaughter was made of the Conmaicni by the foreigners.
807.13: The slaughter of Calraighe Luirg by the Ui Briuin.
807.14: A slaughter was made of the Ui Mic Uais by the Corca Roidhe of Meath.
807.15: A slaughter was made of the foreigners by Cobhthach, son of Maelduin, lord of Loch Lein.

The Annals of the Four Masters were put together in the seventeenth century, but they still give an idea of how much blood was being spilled on both the Viking and Irish sides. This is one of the aspects of raiding life that is generally overlooked in popular culture. Raiding was a hazardous occupation and wherever the

Vikings made camp, they must have been under constant threat of attack by the natives.

By 807, the Vikings were in Donegal and heading down the west coast, where they reached Kerry by 813 and Cape Clear—the southernmost point of Ireland—by 820. They continued to run into trouble. In 811, according to the annals, a number of Vikings were slaughtered in Ulster, and the following year a party was defeated in Mayo.

It was worth it, though. Raiding quickly became a capitalist venture. At the monasteries, the raiders would have found food stocks for their more immediate needs, but for their longer-term aims there would have been treasures such as book covers, chalices, shrines and jewellery. As non-Christians, they clearly had no interest in the objects' religious significance and cared only for their value in the home market. If a raid had been particularly profitable, it wasn't unusual for chalice jewels to end up in the necklaces of a warrior's girlfriend.

With the Vikings came a trend towards using silver as a good way of denoting wealth. Silver could be carried easily, and hidden effectively. A little too effectively, as it turned out. Over 100 silver hoards, dating from between 800 and 1000, have been found in Ireland, having been hidden but never reclaimed. Booty that was chopped up is now referred to as hacksilver, and it forms a decent proportion of the unearthed hoards discovered since, along with jewellery and ingots.

The richest of the Irish monasteries was actually off the west coast of Scotland on Iona, which became a regular target for raiders. During one attack, 68 monks were killed at a place now known as the Bay of the Martyrs, although they may have been fighting back at the time.

Following several raids on Iona, the Vikings returned in 825, this time looking for a shrine to the settlement's founder, St Columba. Having had advance warning, the monks buried the shrine. They had been ordered to do so by the settlement's leader,

Blathmac, a former warrior of noble blood. It is said that Blathmac had originally gone to Iona in a calculated attempt to gain martyrdom at the hands of the Vikings. If so, his elaborate suicide bid proved to be a triumph. When he refused to reveal the shrine's whereabouts, the Vikings tortured Blathmac to death, tearing him 'limb from limb' according to a contemporary account. He finished up a saint as a result.

The abbot of Iona had already fled a couple of decades earlier, to Kells in Meath where a new monastery was established. He took many of the island's treasures with him. Among these was The Book of Kells, for which academics and the Irish tourist industry are eternally grateful.

The Viking fleets became bigger as the ninth century wore on, so that in 837 a fleet of 60 ships is described as appearing on the Boyne river in Louth, and perhaps the same fleet then made its way down the east coast. The sight of it must have been both spectacular and not a little unnerving to the Irish living in small settlements along the shoreline.

Over time, the Vikings ventured farther inland, up the rivers Shannon and Liffey, up the Boyne into Meath and the Vartry in Wicklow. As their attacks grew in intensity, they eventually realised that there was no longer any point in raiding during the summer and returning home for the winter.

In 840, a Viking fleet became the first to stay out the winter in Ireland when its sailors camped at Lough Neagh, in the north. The following year, they built a longphort—a sheltered defensive stronghold with immediate access to the sea—in Co. Louth. And that same year, a Viking fleet journeyed farther south along the east coast, entered a wide bay and sailed upriver. They either spotted an area they thought useful for building a longphort, or they just attacked and grabbed an existing defensive site from some natives. The result was the same. The Vikings had founded Dublin.

———

If you are ever in the vicinity of Dublin's Christ Church Cathedral, it's worth taking a small diversion to Fishamble Street. It curves behind the unloveable trilogy of slabs that form the Civic Offices, halting at the bank of the Liffey, where Essex Quay meets Wood Quay. In recent years, businesses and the City Council have refurbished the area around it in the hope of enticing Dubliners, and tourists, just that bit farther west along the river. It has only been partially successful because it remains in a part of Dublin that, while within a few minutes' stroll of the very centre of the city, feels somewhat overlooked. Much of Fishamble Street is now nothing more than a throughway. Even still, many Dubliners will have never sloped through it.

There is a historical monument there, a granite slab to the first public performance of George Frideric Handel's *Messiah*, which took place at noon on Tuesday, 13 April 1792 at Neale's Music Hall on the street. Into the hall squeezed 700 men (asked, due to the restricted space, to attend without their swords) and 300 women (without their hoops) for a near-riotous occasion. The site later became home to a small steel factory, which was demolished in the late 1990s and replaced by apartments, accessed through the original entrance to that music hall. A hotel is named after the composer; a plaque and graffiti-blotted inscription mark the production of the *Messiah*. It has even spawned an annual week-long Handel festival in the city each April.

Yet, a stroll down to the end of the street hints at a more ancient history. There, on Essex Quay, a sculpture of a half-sunken Viking ship sits beside a bus stop. But the boat has a better claim to be there, because the Liffey's banks were once wide, shallow and flooded at this point and beyond. And the boat is a reminder of why Fishamble Street once amounted to much more than the site of a demolished music hall.

Over a thousand years ago, the bottom of this street once connected to a busy dock from which fish was unloaded from Viking ships and brought to the shops—the 'fish shambles'—that gave the street its name. There were jewellers here too, and woodcarvers and various other merchants, in buildings squeezed onto plots, their entrances set back from a street laid down with wooden logs.

The smell would have been quite astonishing to the modern nose—open cesspits in front yards filled with human waste, fish remains, whatever bits of a slaughtered cow or pig weren't required. At the docks at Wood Quay, the odours would have been of more than just fish, but also of turpentine, tar, seasoned oak, the spices being unloaded and the faeces from animals such as ponies.

A short walk south would probably have brought you to the king's residence at what became Dublin Castle, although it would have been a modest building—larger than the other residences but little more than a defended thatched house. There was a network of streets nearby, with the comb-makers and leather workers on High Street and metal workers at Christchurch Place.

To its east there was a parliament, or Thingmote, up a small hill by Trinity College, at roughly the spot where the church on Andrew Street stands now. Farther east was the Stein, a long stone placed at where Pearse Street now meets D'Olier Street, but which was then a tidal strand where the Vikings would have pulled up their boats. That stone, perhaps 14 ft high and unmarked, survived until as recently as the seventeenth century when it was removed to make way for development. A replica stands there now.

A thousand years ago, Ireland was an economic hub, through which passed people and goods flowing from Scandinavia into western Europe and towards Africa, and it made Dublin a town of dizzying importance. That it was a town at all was something of a novelty in a country of monastic settlements and scattered farmsteads. Settlements in Ireland were spaced out and extended families often lived in forts. There were promontory forts, built on land jutting out over the sea, so clearly easier to defend, and there were the more common circular ringfort farmsteads, which were surrounded by a bank of earth and sometimes stones to make for better defence against raiders and against wild animals, such as wolves.

The ringforts would often be sites of continuous habitation through generations, so that successive structures were built after the previous was razed and covered with clay. Their remnants still litter the Irish countryside; an estimated 40,000 of them have been identified. Despite their being under constant threat of modern development, and that new ones are still being found, only about 200 have been excavated, and many of those which have been examined have turned out not to be ringforts at all. One supposed ringfort actually proved to be a circle of trees made as a nineteenth-century landscaping feature.

The ringforts would occasionally have been accompanied by souterrains, man-made caves. Their construction was sometimes simple, involving a tunnelling of the clay or soft rock. But they could also be quite ingenious, such as those dug into the raised parts of the ringforts and which often sprouted off into separate hallways and chambers. A really impressive example at Donaghmore, near Dundalk, Co. Louth runs for a total of about 70 m, contains about five passages at a couple of levels, and had ventilation shafts designed into walls that still hold their shape despite it being maybe a thousand years or more since the tunnel was first dug.

Souterrains would have had a variety of uses. While they would have been convenient for storing food, their complexity has led to speculation that they may have been used as hiding places during battles or raids. They may sometimes have proven more of a danger than a sanctuary. If the refugees were discovered, the tunnels would have been easily dug into. Worse, enemies could have used smoke either to force out those huddling inside or to suffocate them.

The Vikings altered the rural pattern of Irish settlement for good. It didn't happen immediately—towns took centuries to catch on across the country—and the idea of people clustering together in urban formation wasn't the Vikings' alone. There is a fierce academic debate about what exactly constitutes a town in the medieval period, but it has been argued that the monasteries functioned as proto-towns, attracting settlement and cottage industries. When they became involved in various fights, the monastic settlements were sizeable enough that large armies could be drawn from the population, and large casualties resulted. If the numbers outlined in the annals are to be trusted, then 1,000 were killed or taken prisoner during a Viking raid on Armagh on 869. In 951, a raid on Kells is recorded as taking 3,000 people. These are astonishing figures for any age and emphasise the size of these places.

Cork can make a claim to be the oldest urban settlement in the country, developing along the banks of the Lee in the seventh and eighth centuries in response to the growth of a local monastery and eventually being settled by the Vikings. But urbanisation didn't trouble most of the island. Ireland would remain a rural country for centuries to come, and recent evidence suggests that even small groups of Vikings lived in rural settlements in places, such as Kerry, with which they are not traditionally associated.

The resistance the Vikings faced in the north seems to have made it more difficult for them to gain a foothold in that part of the island. In fact, some have speculated that the Vikings' ultimate failure to establish themselves in the north eventually put that region at a long-term economic disadvantage. Because where they did settle down and begin trading, the Vikings brought wealth to themselves and, in time, to those surrounding them.

Along the east and south coasts of the country, the Vikings developed large towns from their longphorts: Dublin's founding in 841 was followed by a camp at Cork in 848; Waterford was established sometime before 860; Limerick before 887; Wexford before 892. Of that list, only Wexford is not now one of the Republic of Ireland's six legally-defined cities (Kilkenny and Galway are the others with that honour).

When the Vikings first arrived in Dublin in 841, they were not the first to have noticed its suitability for settlement. Mesolithic and Neolithic people had previously taken advantage of both the sea and the farmland, and the streets on which the Vikings developed the city were themselves traced along ancient routes.

So, when the Vikings arrived, it was to an area that already had distinct communities. On the north bank, to the east of modern-day Usher's Island, a settlement had formed at the meeting of three ancient routeways at a crossing point, hence the name Áth Cliath ('ford of the hurdles'). It was needed, because crossing the Liffey could be treacherous. In 770, soldiers of an Irish army are said to have drowned trying to cross a river that in Irish was known as *Ruirthech*, meaning 'tempestuous'.

On the south bank, at a pool formed by the meeting of the Liffey and a tributary, the Poddle, was a monastic settlement. To the native Irish, it was *Duiblinn*, the 'black pool', and the Vikings adopted the name, altering it to *Dyflinn*. It is this that leads many historians to believe that they first settled at the pool, although the archaeological evidence isn't there to back it up. A compromise of sorts can be found today in how both settlements live on in the city's names: *Baile Áth Cliath* in Irish; Dublin in English.

If you stand on Dublin's quays today, the concrete and tar of the city's streets disguise the natural topography that the Vikings would have encountered. You need to try to scrub them from your mind and concentrate instead on the way in which the land south of the Liffey slopes steeply upwards. The Liffey has been narrowed substantially since the arrival of the Vikings, and several of its tributaries, including the Poddle, have been diverted beneath the city's streets. The original streets, including Fishamble Street, climbed up from the salt marshes and sandbanks of the Liffey, which had a broad tidal channel that went 3 km upriver as far as Islandbridge.

From the moment they first camped by the Liffey, the Vikings used their new base to launch raids on the immediate area. As they plundered inland, they also began to trade with Viking settlements on the west coast of Britain, and the urban outpost established itself in such a way that it began to attract women, either local or Scandinavian, to join the men who were the initial raiders. They were, however, politically smart. By the 850s, the Dublin Vikings already had a king who had married into an Irish family. Irish kings also used Viking mercenaries.

It's easy to imagine that just because we know them collectively as Vikings they were united, but even as they used their base to raid the surrounding area they showed what would be an enduring capacity to fight amongst themselves. The first Vikings to settle in Dublin were Norse, but the 850s saw regular battles between them and Danish Vikings, with control of Dublin see-sawing between either faction.

The locals distinguished between the two not by nationality, of course, but by their appearance. The Norse were the *Finngaill* ('fair foreigners') and the Danes the *Dubhgaill* ('dark foreigners').

Despite all of this, the Vikings set about turning Dublin into the island's most important port and capital. It made it a regular venue for battles, and in 902 the Viking leadership was actually run out of town by Irish raiders, returning as an invasion force in 917. By then, though, they had been living in the area for a couple of generations and most of the Viking residents had no intention of moving. Because, while the Vikings are remembered mainly as expert pillagers, in Dublin they demonstrated the entrepreneurial zeal that was their greatest strength.

To understand why Dublin became so important, it's worth listening to the advice of Dr Patrick Wallace, director of the National Museum of Ireland, which is that you first have to invert your geographical view. Instead of seeing Dublin as a town on the east coast of Ireland, think of it as being on the western shores of the Irish Sea. This was a region into which great Viking fleets poured. These ships carried fighting men, their treasures and their slaves. Goods flowed in and out of Ireland on an unprecedented scale. Major imports included wine, silk, salt and iron, while bone and antler combs, metalwork and jewellery were exported. The city, though, only thrived in the first place because it was built on one industry above all others: slavery.

They didn't bring it to Ireland. Just as they had been raiding monasteries before the Vikings arrived, the Irish were no strangers to the slave trade. It had thrived for several centuries, otherwise the young Welshman who would later become known as St Patrick would not have been brought to the island several hundred years previously.

Patrick, along with many of the early Christians, was grabbed by pagan Irish raiders who had taken advantage of the withdrawal of Roman rule along the west coast of fifth-century Britain. If the Irish would come to dread the arrival of Viking longships on their shores, so the Britons of earlier centuries had feared the cruelty of the Irish slavers who derived so much from the slave trade that in the early years of Christianity, the female slave—the *cumal*—was actually treated as a basic unit of currency in Ireland, used to value fines, land and sometimes a person's life.

Female slaves were important in a way that adult males were not. A male slave—a *mug*—came bottom of the value chain, with young men or boys of greater value. A *cumal*, on the other hand, was worth 3 oz of silver. Alternatively, they were worth between 6 and 8 *seoit* (a *set* being worth between 3 and 8 cows). They would be used in murder trials, so that the freedom of a man could be bought for 7 *cumala*. An item could be bought for half a *cumal*, although this didn't require halving a person but interpreting it as worth 1½ oz of silver or a similar equivalent. Alternatively, a slave could just be rented out for a certain amount of time.

The Vikings, then, did not create the slave trade, although by the time they arrived the Christian people they encountered found it increasingly unpalatable. From early on, however, the Vikings were interested in people almost as much as their silver. We can't always be sure of their motives. There was a 'great prey of women' taken at Howth, Co. Dublin in 821. Why they were grabbed is unsure. Given the toll generally wreaked upon women during warfare, it's possible that they would have been subjected to terrible ordeals by men who had been away from home for a considerable length of time. However, as was the case in the Irish slave system, women were counted the most valuable of all hostages.

At the beginning, the Vikings would most likely have kidnapped for ransom, with kings and their families taken for financial motives. There would have been limits on how many slaves could be trafficked at any one time, given that the boats could only hold so many people. Gradually, though, Dublin developed as the centre of the Viking slave trade, rivalled in its importance only by Bristol on the British west coast. From these ports, the Vikings operated a market that stretched all the way to the Mediterranean.

They traded with merchants as far south as Spain, who in turn would trade some of those slaves farther south, so that many northern European slaves ultimately found themselves at work in the dusty heat of north Africa. Often, the Vikings would simply raid an area close to the market they wished to trade with. They took Scandinavians—fair-haired women being particularly valuable—and sold them on to the highest bidder, sometimes sending slaves on a journey through many owners, across thousands of miles. A Viking might sell on to a Jewish trader who might in turn sell on to a Muslim trader. There are stories of 'bright-fleshed' young boys and girls appearing in homosexual and heterosexual harems in Muslim lands.

Meanwhile, slaves landed in Ireland from great distances away, so that there is a description of 'blue men' arriving in the country in the ninth century, possibly African slaves or defeated Spanish moors. They were of such note that the name has stuck. *Fear gorm* ('blue man') remains a common Irish-language term for 'black man'.

If you were taken as a slave, you could largely abandon hope of ever seeing home or family again. And the chances of being born into slavery, or forced into it, were significant. The population of western Europe by 950 has been estimated at about 22 million, and the conservative guess is that 15 per cent of these were slaves.

It's an extraordinary figure, meaning that, if you had the misfortune to be alive in these exciting but dangerous times, you had almost a one in six chance of being a slave. The odds could be worse depending on where you happened to have been born. In eleventh-century Britain, the population of the western part of the country is estimated to have comprised about 20 per cent slaves.

The word 'slave', by the way, comes from the Vikings' success in capturing people from the Slavic countries to their east. The Slavics would eventually get revenge of sorts when the Viking empire waned in the twelfth century and there were successful counter-raids on the Scandinavian lands. In 1135, one Slavic raid on Gothenburg bagged a reported 7,000 hostages (that figure is disputed), all of whom were sold into slavery.

By the eleventh century, as the Vikings of Dublin gradually converted to Christianity, slavery became a less acceptable trade. Besides, there wasn't much new territory to conquer and so fewer people to take. By then, the Irish had been scattered across the territories. For instance, the colonisation of Iceland saw the migration of so many Irish that it left a deep imprint on that island's genetic stock.

Although, the first thing the Vikings had to do when they got to Iceland was kick a few Irish off the island. About one-fifth bigger than Ireland, Iceland had no natives as such when the Vikings began to inhabit it during the late 800s. But it did have a smattering of Irish monks who had rowed all that way in currachs in search of a bit of peace and quiet and a suitably austere existence.

One Irish monk, Dicuil, had even been the first person to write of Iceland's existence. An impressively learned man, Dicuil's career highlights included writings on astronomy and the demolition of the western world's widely held belief that elephants couldn't lie down. He was also an extensive traveller and, while he had never visited Iceland himself, in an 825 work, *Liber de mensura orbis terrae*, he described meeting with several monks who, some 30 years previously, claimed to have lived on a northern island called Thule. This is probably a reference to Iceland.

Irish monks almost certainly travelled to Iceland as anchorites, religious hermits who sought the most extreme solitude and harshest conditions in which to live. And they could hardly have got more extreme than a volcanically active, treeless island with few native species and a winter that brought only a few dim hours of daylight. The summers were so bright, explained Dicuil, that even at night, 'A man can do whatever he wishes, even pick the lice from his shirt, as if it were broad daylight.'

Irish monks left behind no archaeological remnants, only circumstantial evidence of their having been there. An early Icelandic historian, the aptly named Ari the Learned, wrote, 'There were Christian men here then, whom the Norsemen called "Papar" [the Norse word for the Irish monks], but they went away for they did not want to live amongst heathen men; and behind them they left bells, books and crosiers.'

They also, it seems, left place names. Papey is on the south-east coast of Iceland, as is Papafjord and Papataettur ('the ruins of the Papar'). More literally, there is Irskishollur, 'the Irishman's hillock'.

The Vikings' colonisation of Iceland, though, brought a great many Irish, not all of them thanks to slavery. Others went as emigrants. By the mid-900s, there would have been enough inter-marriage between Irish and Vikings that, as the settling of Iceland began, many of them and their new families decided to try out life on the island.

As for those Irish who were taken there as slaves, they are described as having been (understandably) surly and unco-operative. Regardless of how they got there, though, a lot of Gaelic women went to Iceland. Scandinavian historians had long wondered if most Icelandic women should be able to trace a Gaelic ancestry; either Irish or, thanks to other Viking settlements, Scottish. It turns out that they can. Genetic research tells us that about half of modern Icelandic women have Gaelic ancestry. Meanwhile, about a quarter of Icelandic men have Gaelic origins.

So, large numbers of people would have come in and out of the Vikings' Irish ports, heading to all corners of Europe. There were traders, mercenaries, migrants and slaves. The human traffic meant that Dublin developed relatively quickly and by the tenth century goods were entering and leaving Ireland on an unrivalled scale.

Boats of various sizes crowded the wharves along the Liffey. Trading ships, which had rooms, including a large middle room big enough to take cargo, would have been able to sail for longer. The warships were long and narrow with shallow hulls, so they could be sailed towards shore and dragged onto land. There were benches for rowers when the winds were not strong enough to sail. Some boats were built in Dublin—there was a shipyard in Temple Bar—but the city also became a hub at which boats would stock up on provisions on their way to other lands.

Out of the country went hunting dogs, hides, wool and mercenaries, on hired fleets, who would embark on foreign military adventures at the right price. In came wine, fur, silver, horses from Britain, silks, Arctic furs, plums from southern England, walnuts from the Continent, amber from the Baltic, walrus ivory from the north Atlantic and ponies from Wales. In the process, Dublin became greatly developed. By the 1100s, a town that had only recently been a very small pair of settlements had become a rich and thriving port.

Markets would have developed in each of the Viking towns, to which the native Irish would travel. Urban areas were also responsible for creating new markets in their hinterlands, which in turn may have afforded their inhabitants protection from raids.

Having started off by raiding the religious settlements in the area around them, the Vikings ended up bringing these same settlements into their economic sphere.

It meant that animals were herded in from outside Dublin, for their nutrition, bones and hides. Timber was needed for construction, while land was needed to farm the food. We know that strawberries, cherries, plums, apples, blackberries, rowans, sloes and hazelnuts were brought to Dublin to be eaten. And we know that there was an important market in moss, because this is what Vikings used as toilet paper.

Dublin's Viking kings had some delightfully evocative nicknames. There was Sihtric Caoch, which translated as 'Squinty'. There was an 'Iron Knee' who was murdered by a servant and replaced by Sitric Silkbeard, who was king when the Vikings fought at the Battle of Clontarf in 1014.

There was an influential ninth-century king, Ivar the Boneless, who was so-named, it seems, because of some disability that required he be carried everywhere. Ivar's brothers included 'White Shirt', Bjorn 'Ironside' and Sigurd 'Snake-Eye'. All were sons of Ragnar 'Hairy Trousers', who got his name thanks to the improvised armour he was once reputed to have sported.

Several of the kings of Dublin were also kings of York in England, illustrating the strong links either side of the Irish Sea. Viking coins minted in Ireland from 997 onwards were acceptable currency in both islands. In fact, as the Viking settlements quickly became independent, although they remained strongly plugged into the economy of the Viking world, after a time there was no central homeland to which they immediately turned.

It meant that when the Irish attacked and forced out Dublin's Viking leadership in 902, the refugees fled not to Scandinavia but to Britain, from where they plotted their eventual return. There, they displayed their capacity for internecine strife. Refugees from Dublin had settled near Chester on land given to them by a female ruler, Aethelflaed. Five years later, they turned on her and attacked

Newgrange, Co. Louth, the most recognisable structure built by the Neolithic culture that introduced farming to Ireland. (*David Lyons / Alamy*)

The piece of flint found at Mell, Co. Louth, and which is the oldest artefact found in Ireland, which was carried by a glacial sheet. (*National Museum of Ireland*)

Mount Sandel finds which, along with those at Lough Boora, come from the earliest known habitat. (*Professor Peter Woodman 2009. Photograph reproduced courtesy of the Trustees of National Museums Northern Ireland*)

Johann Georg Ramsauer, salt-mine manager, father of 22 children, and a very important amateur archaeologist. (*Wikimedia Commons*)

Graves in Hallstatt, Austria, as examined by Johann Georg Ramsauer, but drawn in great detail by Isidor Engel during the 1870s. (*Mary Evans*)

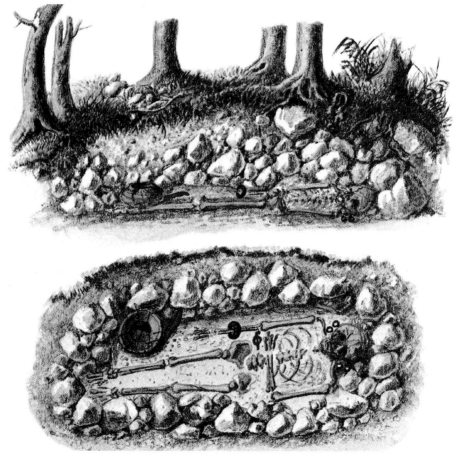

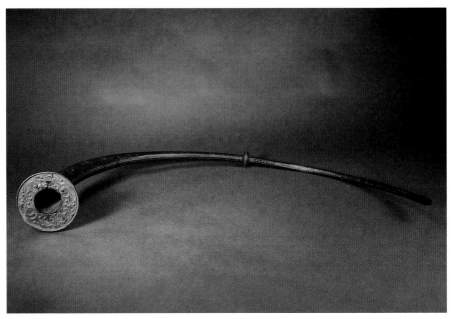

Loughnashade Trumpet, held by the National Museum. (*National Museum of Ireland*)

'The Dying Gaul', while a Roman copy of an earlier sculpture, shows how the Romans saw nobility in their foe. (*Peter Barritt / Alamy*)

Sea Stallion, a replica Viking longship that sailed from Roskilde, Denmark, to Dublin and back again during 2007 and 2008. (*Imagefile*)

Viking helmets. Note the total absence of horns. (*Troy GB Images / Alamy*)

The sculpture of the sunken Viking boat at Wood Quay, Dublin, which reminds passers-by that it was once a bustling hub of the Scandinavian empire. (*imagebroker / Alamy*)

A board game found at Ballinderry, Co. Westmeath. The Vikings loved board games, and even created travel versions to keep themselves busy on long journeys. (*National Museum of Ireland*)

Modern Icelandic people, whose genetic make-up is heavily influenced by the Gaelic migrants who arrived when the Vikings settled the island. (*Getty Images*)

The reconstructed effigy of Strongbow at Christ Church Cathedral, alongside an effigy of his son who, contrary to popular myth, was not cut in half by his father. (*Topfoto*)

'The Marriage of Strongbow and Aoife'. He was promised her hand in return for helping Dermot MacMurrough regain power in Leinster, so triggering the Norman invasion. (*National Gallery of Ireland*)

A corner of the National Museum of Ireland gives us a glimpse of medieval life in Ireland. (*National Museum of Ireland*)

Oliver Cromwell, whose military victory over Irish Catholics triggered an unprecedented shift in land ownership. (*Philip Mould Ltd, London / The Bridgeman Art Library*)

Rathlin Island, off Co. Antrim, where it is likely that the Vikings first landed in Ireland. (*Kevin Dwyer*)

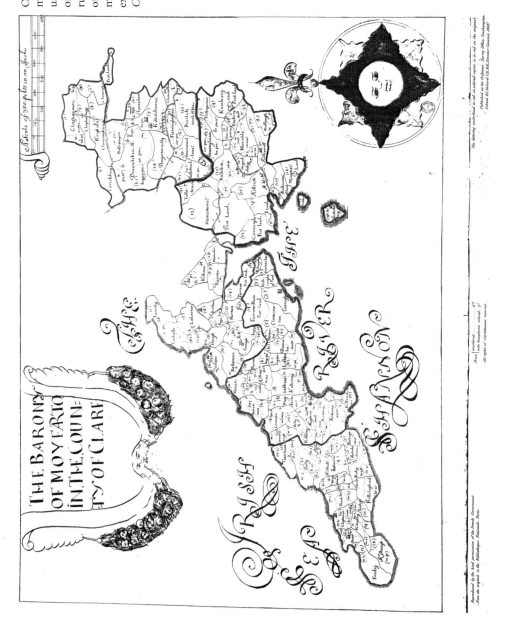

One of William Petty's maps of Ireland. Made by using soldiers with free time on their hands and a rudimentary understanding of taking measurements, the maps provided extraordinary detail. (*Clare County Library*)

The Huguenot cemetery off St Stephen's Green in Dublin is a reminder of the small but significant influx of Protestant refugees into Ireland during the eighteenth century. (*Topfoto*)

Palatine, Co. Carlow, named after a small migration of German Protestants who arrived there in the early eighteenth century. (*Wikimedia Commons*)

Dublin's Jewish Lord Mayor, Robert Briscoe, having tea at the Jewish school in 1957. The Jewish community in Dublin was sizeable enough for a 'Little Jerusalem' to develop.

Mosney, Co. Meath: once a holiday camp until it became Ireland's largest centre for asylum seekers.

Brazilians enjoy a carnival in Gort, Co. Galway. By 2006, 40 per cent of the town had not been born in Ireland. (*Connacht Tribune. Photo by Joe O'Shaughnessy*)

Moore Street market, still symbolic of old Dublin, but now energised by the immigrant shops and shoppers. (RTÉ *Stills*)

By 2006, Polish was the unofficial second language of Ireland, spoken daily by more people than used Irish.

Chester, only to be held off by her army. They were not quite the ideal guests.

In Ireland, the Vikings also showed a repeated capacity to fight among themselves. As they set about establishing settlements in Dublin, Waterford and Limerick within a short time of each other they might then have gone about forming strong trade links and allegiances. Actually, a turf war broke out, with various Viking groups trying to establish areas from which they could raid freely. The Vikings of Limerick (also a sizeable slaving port) and Dublin shared a notable animosity, and it was the Dubliners' eventual military triumph that helped establish the town as the de facto capital of the country. Meanwhile, during such power struggles among the Vikings, the Irish would take advantage by launching attacks.

Despite all that scrapping, the Vikings did not take control of the entire island. There remains some debate about whether they ever intended to. It has been argued that they were never interested in seizing land as such, but in establishing trading posts for their maritime empire. However, others have suggested that they did not conquer Ireland only because their attempts failed. They had landed in an Ireland that had a hierarchy of kings—usually with the King of Tara at the top—and power was handed down through a dynasty and was not something that could be simply seized and then assigned to whoever wanted it.

Even if they didn't have ambitions to take the entire island, the Vikings would have discovered the difficulties of trying to take even parts of it and they spent much of their time defending, losing or regaining their Irish territory.

Fights would have been brutal and bloody. Those who died in battle would have left this world in a decidedly horrible fashion, while those who were only badly wounded might have wished they were dead, because medicine was—to put in mildly—rudimentary. There was no anaesthetic. Any surgery on embedded arrowheads, amputations and the like would have been done with the aid of a rope to tie the poor victim down. If a rope was unavailable, then a few strong helpers would have had to grab and hold him down.

A clean blade would not have caused the worst wound compared with a barbed blade, which would have been horribly difficult to remove. The answer was to shove it through the wound to the other side. If the blade was wedged in the shoulder, this would have been a particularly nasty procedure.

If splinters from the wood were lodged in the flesh too, a bit more rooting around would have been required to pick them out. Any stitching (if the patient was lucky) would first involve piercing holes in the skin large enough for a bone needle and linen to pass through. If needle and thread were not available, then cauterisation would be the alternative, meaning that if you hadn't passed out from the pain of being stabbed by the sword, then the red-hot irons would do the trick. And in an era of herbal medicines, an infected wound could be deadly.

In 1879, while clearing a mound in Donnybrook, about 5 km south of Dublin City, workmen uncovered a skeleton. Then another. Then another until about 600 skeletons had been revealed to the elements.

We'll never know the exact number of skeletons, or when they were put there, because aside from the visits of gentlemen anti-quarians, no formal archaeological dig was carried out. Instead, the bones and tools were dispersed without being recorded. Few of them remain, although a spindle whorl (for spinning yarn), a bone comb and a fragment of flint now rest in the National Museum of Ireland. A sword—severely damaged, but with an elaborately decorated hilt—also appears to have survived, some-how passing into private hands and eventually arriving in a Nottingham museum, where it has been on display since 1964.

The Donnybrook grave contained all sections of a popu-lation—from foetuses to the elderly—but featured two layers. In the bottom layer, skeletons were deliberately spaced, in two rows, with heads facing west and feet to the east. The layer above that, however, had no order to it. Bodies were thrown in at random. Most of its inhabitants had died young, some had severe wounds, and several piles of skulls were found some distance from the other corpses. It looked as if it was a mass grave, filled after a massacre.

The most important resident of the grave was clearly a warrior, killed by a blow that pierced his forehead. On one side of him was a sword, and on the other a spearhead, and it would seem this Viking had been buried in a pre-existing Irish grave, perhaps as a posthumous symbol of supremacy.

What is so important about this find is that it was among a handful of burial sites discovered during the nineteenth century, after which nothing else was found for over a century. However, as recently as 2003, half a skeleton was discovered on South Great George's Street, in Dublin's city centre. His shield on his chest, and his knife by his side, it's likely that he once had a sword by his right side. It followed the discovery the previous year of another single burial. Both were close to the original 'black pool', and three other burials were subsequently discovered in the area.

It's unsurprising that the graves repeatedly reveal warriors. According to the laws of the period, all freemen were expected to own weapons. However, at graves found in Kilmainham and Islandbridge archaeologists also discovered farming tools, weighing scales and other goods alongside the weapons, showing us that Viking life wasn't all about raiding.

Death at the point of a sword, while not uncommon, was certainly not the biggest worry. Anyone living beyond their 50s in this era would have had a good innings. Women regularly died in childbirth. Whatever about battle, arthritis would have been a significant problem for those used to the hard work of tending a farm or scrap of land. Leprosy, typhus and smallpox would have been common killers, although a big threat would have been dysentery caused by the lack of sanitation. In 951, we know that there was a great outbreak of leprosy and dysentery in Dublin (the same year, incidentally, in which the Annals of Ulster describe 'a great mortality of bees').

The Vikings did, at least, have good teeth. Graves show few cavities, thanks to the absence of white sugar in their diet.

If a child was born healthy, it had a substantial chance of dying before its fifth birthday. The children who did survive played with toys such as the small wooden boats that have turned up at archaeological sites, and would also have played with model animals and miniature weapons.

We've a fairly good idea of how much the adults enjoyed board games. A popular game at the time was *Hnefa-tafl*, or 'King's Table', which had been played since AD 400, and which the Vikings eventually carried as far west as Greenland and east to the Ukraine. *Tafl* is the Old Norse word for table, so that by the end of the Viking period, many games came with that adjunctive. Chess—introduced in the eleventh and twelfth centuries—was *Skak-Tafl* or 'check-table'; Tabula (the medieval ancestor of backgammon) was introduced from the French as *Quatre* and thus *Kvatru-Taf.*

There were regional variations. In Ireland, it was known as *Fitchneal,* and was played on a smaller board than elsewhere, with different starting positions for each player. We're not entirely sure how it was played, as there is no definitive instruction surviving. However, it's generally accepted that it involved two players, with one being the king, who begins at the centre of the board, surrounded by defenders. The king has to reach one of the four corners of the board without being captured by the attackers ranged around its perimeter. Sometimes a dice was used, a game which the Irish called *Brandubh,* or 'black crows'.

Boards varied in size, and were usually wooden. The finest example is a yew board, with 49 squares, found on Ballinderry Crannog, Co. Westmeath in 1936, and which was probably made in Dublin. Showing a penchant for travel board games that predate ours by centuries, the Vikings sometimes drilled holes in the middle of the playing squares, so that the pieces could be pegged in and easily carried around. Game boards were also carved into the bottom of decks, where Vikings would while away the crossings by playing tic-tac-toe.

What they wore while they played is not that clear. Only scraps of Viking clothing have survived the centuries, so that archaeologists have had to be inventive, extrapolating from threads that have survived on brooches and other accessories. From their efforts, we think that some men wore long woollen or linen undershirts with a tunic on top, and a chord or belt around the waist. Others sported rather practical trousers which it is thought the Vikings brought with them. A cloak would have completed the outfit. The women wore long underdresses, and bonnets or scarves on their heads. Shoes took a variety of forms, from ankle boots to slip-ons, fastened by toggles or ties.

It seems that the Vikings would have worn similar clothes regardless of their place in the social pecking order, with wealth being more obvious in the quality and colour of the material, and the accessories. The most expensive fabric, silk, would have been imported to Ireland from as far away as China and Baghdad.

The wealthy, though, would have afforded high quality jewellery, with necklaces sometimes displaying the reach of the Viking culture (they would also have owned coins that were Roman or from other parts of Europe). It influenced how the native Irish indicated their status. Before their arrival, wealth in Ireland had been measured in such ways as heads of cattle. The wearing of silver jewellery gradually became a new way for native Irish to show their riches in a more ostentatious manner.

———

In the end, as the Viking empire waned across Britain and Europe, its people began to blend deeper and deeper into the native population. A heavy defeat at the battle of Tara marked a turning point for the Vikings as a fighting force in Ireland. But it is the Battle of Clontarf on Good Friday of 1014 that is often held up as the moment at which the natives, led by Brian Boru, kicked the Vikings out of the country once and for all. It certainly got some decent write-ups, thanks not only to the *Cogadh*, in which the tale grew significantly in the retelling, but also through Scandinavian texts that added a good deal of exaggeration while also crediting Boru with being a brilliant leader.

In reality, the fight was complex, involving several kings, complicated family links, Vikings and Irish allying with each other and a very messy outcome. It was so messy, in fact, that some historians believe it is more accurate to call it a stalemate than a glorious victory for the Irish.

The Battle of Clontarf was the culmination of a power struggle between Boru, who had ruled most of the country for over a decade and had even gone as far as to crown himself high king, and the King of Leinster, a fellow called Máel Mórda mac Murchada. Key to all of this was Sitric Silkbeard, the Viking King of Dublin. The complexities of the diplomacy are no better illustrated than in how Boru, in an effort to show dominance over his opponents, married Sitric's mother, Gormlaith, who also happened to be mac Murchada's sister. As a way of attempting to influence two branches of a family in one go, it was quite bold. It also happened to be an utter failure.

It was partly because Gormlaith, if accounts are to be believed, was quite the conniver, and not in any way a hapless bargaining chip. History remembers her as having stoked the grievances that led to war between her husband, son and brother. It seems that Brian Boru didn't need any time to decide that she was to blame, because before he left to take on his enemies at Clontarf he locked her up.

On Boru's side were a couple of powerful kings, including Gormlaith's previous husband. Against him was ranged an alliance of forces from Viking Dublin, Leinster, Orkney and the Isle of Man. There were about 5,000 troops on the field. (One recent book, David W. McCullough's *Wars of the Irish Kings*, says that this makes this 'one of the largest battles yet fought in Ireland'. To which the natural response is: *yet?*)

Today, Clontarf is an established and busy suburb of the city. In 1014, it was a marshy field by a small stream and it is thought that the battle would have been witnessed from the city walls. By the time it was fought, Boru was in his 70s and is said to have watched the fighting from a distance. At first he would have been concerned as the Leinster and Viking forces—some in armour—gained the upper hand against his army which did not wear armour but did use shields.

However, as the day wore on, and the battle spread along the edge of the Liffey, Boru's men gradually dominated, sending the Viking force fleeing for their boats only for them to discover that a high tide had carried many of them away.

Famously, Boru was killed in his tent by a fleeing Viking leader, Brodar. The popular depiction of him being stabbed as he prayed may have been an invention to later emphasise his piety. As for Brodar, it was the last act of his life because he was quickly caught and killed.

Dublin did not actually fall to Brian Boru's men, and after he died there was infighting and mutiny among his army, which is why the Battle of Clontarf may not have been the clear-cut victory that it is popularly depicted to be. The Vikings did not, then, up and leave in 1014 any more than they had when Dublin was overrun in 902. Nevertheless, it was the last great battle the Vikings fought in Ireland and was significant enough to effectively mark the end of the Viking Age in Ireland, even if it was part of an ongoing shift in power. Limerick had fallen to the Irish some 50 years before, and Dublin would keep its independence for another 50 years.

Over the course of almost two centuries, the Vikings had become traders, farmers and sailors, as well as husbands and fathers in mixed families. There had been fosterage between Viking and Irish families, in which each other's children were raised together as a way of solidifying allegiances.

The Vikings were no longer pagans but had converted to Christianity. Even though the last Viking raid on Iona occurred almost two centuries after the first, by that stage there were so many Christian Vikings that several had settled and died as penitents on the island.

Even as they began to seep into the demographic background, their influence was proving to be permanent. For instance, the Vikings not only gave Ireland towns but also their names. The prefix -*ford* comes from the Norse *fjord*, and even though Killary in Co. Galway is the only true fjord in Ireland, plenty of towns were given the name anyhow. Waterford was a Norse settlement, and may have got its name from an old word for 'windy ford'. Wexford was a shallow fjord, Strangford referred to the strong current. Carlingford was 'hag's fjord', named, it is believed, after the hills surrounding the town.

Howth is believed to come from the Norse word for headland. Leixlip is the salmon's leap; Oxmanstown, 'the town of the men who came from the east'. In all, there are 78 place names in Ireland that are definitely or possibly of Norse origin.

As the Hiberno-Norse moved from Ireland into Britain, they also left an imprint on the place names there. North-west England is replete with places that either refer to the Irish or are indebted to Old Irish. The Wirral peninsula in Cheshire has Irby ('settlement of the Irish'). Other signs of the migration from Ireland to Britain come in the sculptures, which mix Viking shafts with Celtic crosses and show how, culturally, the Vikings borrowed as much from the Irish as they gave.

The Viking legacy is in the Irish language. There are plenty of Irish words that can be traced to Old Norse. Market in Irish is *margadh*; in Norse it was *markadr*. *Bróg* (shoe) comes from *brok*; *Pinginn* (penny) from *penningr*. The Irish for anchor is *ancaire*, the Norse was *akkeri*. It's no surprise to find that many of the shared words have something to do with seafaring or trade. In English we say boat, in Irish we say *bád*, but the only reason we say either is because of the Old Norse *bátr*.

And the Vikings brought surnames. Quite literally. Surnames were only adopted in Ireland between 900 and 1200, or roughly the period in which the Vikings were most influential. Until then, people had been known as Mac ('son of') or Ó ('grandson/ descendant of'). Some of the surnames we can attach to the Vikings stick with this formula, for instance, *McAuliffe* means 'Son of Olaf' while *McManus* is 'Son of Magnus'. However, others are descriptive. The rather straightforward *Doyle* hides its origins as an Anglicised version of Ó *Dubhghaill*, which literally translates as 'son of the dark foreigner'. *Higgins* originates from the Gaelic word *uigan*, for Norse seaman.

Yet, there remains an enigmatic postscript, because the one thing that they might not have left behind is their genes. In 2005, scientists at the Smurfit Institute of Genetics at Trinity College Dublin decided to examine just how much of a genetic legacy the Vikings bequeathed us. They looked at the genes of a thousand Irish and found that there was little evidence of the Vikings lurking in there. So, they narrowed down the search a bit, concentrating on those with Viking-based surnames, because if any group seemed likely to be linked to the Scandinavians, it would surely be these.

It was a small sample—only 47 men—but the results were stark. In these descendants of the Hiberno-Norse, the Norse element was missing from their genes. There are a few reasons why this might be the case. It might be that, as they travelled south through Britain and into Ireland, the Viking blood was already somewhat diluted by the time it got to Ireland in great numbers. It may be that the Vikings didn't come in the numbers needed to make a significant genetic mark. Or that Viking names don't necessarily mean Viking blood. Or it is possible that the sample was not big enough to give us an accurate result.

Or it may be that the Viking genes were pushed out by what was to follow. Because as the Viking Age ended, there was a population of Norse living in the north of France who were about to set in train a series of invasions that would eventually have a seismic impact on Ireland.

Chapter 4

THEY CAME, THEY SAW, THEY ALMOST CONQUERED: THE NORMANS

L ife was pretty good to Lionel of Antwerp, but it really could have been so much better. Fate had been kind enough to send him into the world in 1338 as the second surviving son of Edward III, a man who would be King of England for 50 years. Even though Lionel was not heir to the throne, there were significant perks nonetheless. Such as when, at the age of just four, he was engaged to be married to Elizabeth de Burgh, the 10-year-old daughter of the Earl of Ulster. When he turned 14, and the marriage was finally consummated, he became the proud owner of a very large chunk of Ireland.

So, he had land, status, a powerful father and he'd married well. Yet, there must have been a moment when Lionel began to realise that his life was destined for repeated anticlimax.

For instance, when Edward III defeated the Scots in 1357, he did his utmost to make Lionel the King of Scotland only for the Scots nobility to block the way, so robbing the young man of his only chance ever to be king of anything.

Edward III had also been responsible for taking on France in what turned out to be the Hundred Years War (which could more accurately be called the '116 Years War'). Fighting in it, Lionel's older brother had earned not only a reputation as an excellent military leader, but also a gallant nickname: the Black Prince. Lionel, though, was not so blessed. In 1359, he rode to war in France alongside his father and three brothers, but the French avoided a pitched battle so Lionel experienced little there other than boredom.

He didn't realise this at the time, but ultimately history wouldn't even remember him as the most famous person in his own house. Among Lionel's staff as he journeyed to France was the young poet Geoffrey Chaucer. Here, at least, Chaucer's adventure was more inglorious than his master's, because he was nabbed by the French while foraging for corn for the horses and was only released several months later once a ransom was paid.

Anyway, in 1361, aged 23 and with glory having thus far left him untroubled, it was time for Lionel to take on a new role. He was sent to sort out the mess in Ireland.

Ireland was a constant irritant to the English. Two centuries earlier, in 1169, it had been invaded and conquered with little resistance, but after all that time they still controlled only parts of the country. The settlers were deeply unhappy not only with this, but also with a Dublin administration that was corrupt and malfunctioning and an English Crown that had shown a pronounced lack of interest in their plight. Plus, there was a creeping fear that the English in Ireland were going native.

So, Lionel was dispatched to put some order on things. He arrived accompanied by a large army and, it would seem, a battalion of interior decorators. During his years in Ireland, much of his time was spent attempting to turn Dublin Castle into a royal court. He renovated buildings, pulled down one house, put up another, restored the roof, and spent a good deal of time planning 'sports and his other pleasures'.

Lionel otherwise engaged himself in a costly military campaign which had few lasting gains. The entire revenues of Ireland's exchequer, and then some, were poured into the war. Lionel's limited abilities as a strategist were best illustrated by his decision to move the office of the exchequer from the relative safety of Dublin to the exposure of Carlow, where the castle became such a regular target for attacks that the outrageous cost of defending it was later compounded by the battle-weary staff's demands for a pay hike.

Lionel, in short, failed in just about everything he did in Ireland. Fed up and frustrated by any attempt to placate the colonists, defeat the natives and generally govern an ungovernable island without the massive army and resources needed to do it, he left Ireland in 1367. It is said that he vowed never to set foot in the country again.

He was true to his word. Now a widower (Elizabeth had died in 1363), he quickly arranged a new marriage with a Milanese noblewoman and set off for Milan accompanied by 457 men and 1,280 horses, stopping for great feasts in Paris and Savoy before finally arriving in Milan in 1368, where two days of balls and general entertainment accompanied the wedding. The dowry included the enormous sum of £200,000, the town of Alba and several castles. At last, things were looking up for Lionel. So, it is a great shame that he should drop dead only months into his marriage. He was only 29. There were strong rumours that he had been poisoned. Possibly by his new father-in-law.

Yet, Lionel was not to be completely forgotten by history, because just before he left Ireland he had been responsible for something quite memorable. He convened a meeting of the Irish Parliament at Kilkenny, and presided over a series of laws that attempted, in detailed terms, to stop those English who had been born in Ireland from becoming Irish. This is known as the Statute of Kilkenny.

The Statute was 36 articles intended to 'ordain and establish' English behaviour in Ireland, and prevent the colonists from being sucked into the culture of the 'evil doer' Irish. It decreed that colonists should speak only English and use English names. They must avoid intermarriage or adopting Irish children. The new colonisers and Irish-born English were to be treated equally, and the latter should no longer be insulted as an 'English hobbe' or 'Irish dog'. The English must not ride a horse bareback. To play hurling—a game with 'great sticks and a ball upon the ground, from which great evils and maims have arisen'—was punishable by imprisonment. The Statute also banned them from playing 'coiting', possibly a form of curling then popular among the Scots Gaelic. Instead, they should practise 'gentlemanlike' games such as throwing lances and drawing bows.

They were forbidden from allowing 'pipers, story-tellers, bablers, rimers, mowers, nor any other Irish agent' among the English in case they turned out to be up to no good. 'Rimers' were bards or minstrels, particularly dreaded by the colonists, not because a well-crafted song had some terrific power of subterfuge, but because it was thought that bards could evoke strong curses. A powerful satire, it was truly believed, could kill a man.

The Statute was not intended to destroy Irishness, but to defend Englishness. What impact did it have? Almost none at all. The anti-climactic nature of Lionel's life infected the Statute. While bold and memorable, it was really just a reconstituted version of statutes enacted in the previous century, and which would be dragged up again several times over the following couple of centuries. Nor was it enforced, chiefly because it just wasn't practical.

However, it is remembered because it crystallised a policy and an attitude among the English in Ireland, and was the most striking expression of a fear that was repeated time and time again: that the English who went to Ireland had become a 'middle nation'; that they were becoming, in a damning phrase that was never actually used at the time, 'more Irish than the Irish themselves'.

It had been 200 years since the English had invaded, but the island had not truly been conquered. Instead, it appeared that the island was conquering them.

———

The invasion of Ireland took place in 1169, when an exiled King of Leinster, Dermot MacMurrough, fled to England and invited all comers to return to Ireland and help him to regain his throne. Parts of Ireland were the reward. In the end, it resulted in the King of England, Henry II, following those first invaders, and drawing Ireland into a growing kingdom that stretched all the way down the west coast of France. So began an occupation of the island, either totally or partially, that has continued uninterrupted, ever since.

Yet, the invasion was less *by* the English as we might understand it now, and more *from* England. The Statute of Kilkenny contains a hint towards its cultural origins: it was drawn up not in English, but in French.

If the Irish want to blame anyone for the genesis of a lengthy, strife-ridden occupation that has lasted almost a millennium, they might as well look towards France. Although, they could direct a little anger at the Norwegians, or possibly the Welsh, or even Rome. And they could hold over a little disdain for the Flemish while they're at it. And there were, obviously, a few Irish in there too; although history has ensured MacMurrough's supposed betrayal of Ireland has lingered in the collective memory.

It is, though, known generally as the Anglo-Norman invasion. Sometimes, it is referred to as the Cambro-Norman invasion, which is an acknowledgment that most of its leaders came from Wales, so writing a few lines in the very, very short chapter of history that might be titled 'Welsh Imperialism'.

But for the Norman part we need to look towards France, and before that Scandinavia. Because while the invasion is often considered the last of the Norman invasions, it could also be seen as a lasting legacy of the Viking conquests.

The Normans were originally 'Norsemen' who had settled in the part of France we now know as Normandy for this very reason. A fiefdom was created there for Rollo, who was either a

Dane or a Norwegian (historians and relevant countries have long disagreed) and said to have been so big he had to walk because horses couldn't hold him.

Rollo had been among a fleet that may have raided Scotland and Ireland before harassing Paris at the turn of the tenth century and, having gained a taste for the place, later returned in bigger numbers. Although he was subsequently defeated by a French king, Charles the Simple (son of Louis the Stammerer), the Vikings had become such a nuisance that in 911 Charles gave Rollo a large part of the north coast in return for the Norseman's loyalty. Although Rollo expanded his territory over time—the city of Rouen is named after him—this deal essentially marked the end of the Viking raids on France, the founding of Normandy and the beginnings of what would later become the Norman conquests.

Adopting French, converting to Christianity and becoming a vital part of the Church's military force, the Normans showed an immediate prowess for soaking up the culture around them. They also adopted a particular feudal structure, developed cavalry warfare and built a lot of castles, all of which would become trademarks of theirs.

It was as a result of their fervent adoption of Christianity that they began to spread themselves farther, acting as Rome's muscle in power struggles that required intervention. They conquered a sizeable part of southern Italy, most notably Sicily, but they also reached as far as Malta and captured a sliver of north Africa.

Today, they are more popularly associated with their conquest of England at the Battle of Hastings in 1066, aided by a lucky arrow (not so lucky for King Harold, of course). Led by William the Conqueror (known as Guillaume the Bastard before gaining his reputation for conquering and having his name Anglicised), once they established themselves the Normans threw most of the English ruling class off their land, put their own people into the leading administrative and ecclesiastical roles and imposed an effective power structure.

Upon his death in 1087, William was succeeded as King of England by his son William II, who died in 1100 when an arrow pierced his lung during a hunting expedition. His brother Henry I then reigned until 1135, when he collapsed of food poisoning in France, having reportedly eaten a 'surfeit of lampreys' (a jawless parasite fish).

Henry I was followed by the contentious reign of his nephew Stephen, who caused such a split in the family that it resulted in civil war and a period of British history that is not known as The Anarchy for nothing.

Stephen died in 1154, and Henry II, great-grandson of William the Conqueror, came to power. Henry did not have a nickname, but he had titles, and lots of them: King of England, Count of Anjou, Duke of Normandy, Duke of Aquitaine, Duke of Gascony, Count of Nantes. And it was he who would gain the title that most matters to this story: Lord of Ireland.

Henry II's credentials as an Englishman do not hold up to great scrutiny. He understood spoken English, but spoke only French, ruled a great chunk of France and spent most of his reign there. However, he is said to have cared so deeply about his kingdom that he would be 'crucified with anxiety' over crises when they arose. He was also described as being highly intelligent, domineering, quick to anger but a master of the one-liner. He was a hefty fellow, though not, his contemporaries insisted, through lack of exercise. 'His body was stocky, with a pronounced tendency toward fatness, due to nature rather than self-indulgence—which he tempered with exercise,' said Giraldus Cambrensis (Gerald of Wales), a writer who has become central to the telling of the story of the Anglo-Norman invasion of Ireland.

A French contemporary, Peter de Blois, wrote that:

. . . curved legs, a horseman's shins, broad chest, and a boxer's arms all announce [Henry] as a man strong, agile and bold . . .

he never sits, unless riding a horse or eating . . . In a single day, if necessary, he can run through four or five-day marches and, thus foiling the plots of his enemies, frequently mocks their plots with surprise sudden arrivals . . .

Perhaps it was Henry's 'curved legs' that gave him such wander-lust, because he really couldn't stay still for very long. He relaxed by going on long hunts, but was constantly moving about, mean-ing that anyone who wanted to find him had to engage in a hunt of their own.

He had coveted Ireland from the very beginning of his reign, actively considering an invasion. He was not the first Norman to do so, as both William the Conqueror and Henry I had examined the possibility. However, Henry II had gone a step further, making invasion plans only for his scheme to be quashed, somewhat embarrassingly, by his mother, Empress Matilda.

The scheme had not entirely been a waste of time, however, because Henry had initially sought and attained the approval of the first and last English pope, Adrian IV, a figure who, by virtue of a breathtakingly grand bit of church law, was also held to be Lord of All the Islands in the Sea. Naturally, this included Ireland.

Motivated by the growth of power of an increasingly independent Irish Church at the time, Adrian IV approved of Henry's stated intention to go over there, draw his sword and civilise it. The result was the *Laudabiliter*, a document that granted Ireland to Henry II should he wish to take it.

It read:

You have signified to us, our well-beloved son in Christ, that you propose to enter the island of Ireland in order to subdue the people and make them obedient to laws, and to root out from among them the weeds of sin; and that you are willing to yield and pay yearly from every house the pension of one penny to St Peter, and to keep and preserve the rights of the churches in that land whole and inviolate.

A penny a house, then, was deemed the price of Ireland. The Pope, by way of sealing the deal, sent Henry a gold ring set with a large emerald.

There is just one significant caveat regarding the *Laudabiliter*: it may not have existed. Or if it did, it may have been in a different form to how we now know it. No original exists, only versions as relayed by others. And the chief source comes from a man who would do more to create a damaging stereotype of the Irish than perhaps anyone before or since. But we will return to Gerald of Wales a little later.

Regardless of its provenance, it seems that Henry believed he had his justification, if not his mother's blessing. Still, he was not adverse to the opportunity to revive the plan. So he would have been more than mildly curious when, during a visit to Aquitaine in 1167, he received word that an Irish king, Dermot MacMurrough, had requested a meeting.

MacMurrough had fled his kingdom of Leinster in August 1166 and gone in search of Henry in the hope of persuading him to invade Ireland alongside him. You might presume it would be relatively easy, even in medieval Europe, to track down a barrel-chested, gregarious leader of an empire but, as we've seen, Henry was a hard man to find. It meant that MacMurrough had spent several months roaming England and France in search of him. He had crossed England, travelled through Aquitaine, headed further south into France and then doubled back on himself. Eventually, he found Henry all the way back in Aquitaine. How frustrating it would have been if the English king had refused him an audience.

Henry, though, was amenable, and so it was that one of the most important meetings in Irish history took place. MacMurrough offered his allegiance to Henry in return for an army that would invade Ireland, give him back his kingdom and destroy his rival, the High King of Ireland, Rory O'Connor.

Henry said no. Distracted by problems within his kingdom, he felt he could not afford to divert forces to Ireland. However, Henry gave MacMurrough a letter in which he gave his blessing to anyone who wanted to assist him in his mission. So, the Leinsterman began the long journey northwards, back across the English Channel, into England and then west towards Wales in search of an army.

MacMurrough's meeting with Henry had been only a partial success. It might have been even less successful if he had included one important detail of the story: he had left Ireland because, among other things, there had been a bit of a row over a woman.

———

What had life been like before the Normans pitched up? Well, power struggles had indeed convulsed much of Ireland before their arrival, but although the invaders would later depict the island as isolated and uncivilised, it had actually been engaged with the outside world. The ports had been busy, and the links with Norman England were strong, mainly because the Viking era had ensured that there was regular trade between Ireland and Britain that didn't cease simply because Viking power had waned.

Archaeologists have learned of this because at the time rubbish was very often just tipped over Dublin's city walls, which must have been quite appalling then but has proved quite useful since. Excavations have found red-painted Normandy wares, evidence of trade with the Normans for a couple of centuries before they landed as conquerors. There was also a group of Bristol merchants living in Dublin before 1169, so Ireland was already home to at least a few English.

In Gaelic Ireland, though, the native Brehon laws remained central to society. They governed medicine, property, status and crimes including murder. Looking at them now, they suggest a swinging set, liberal in their attitudes to marriage and sex; far more liberal, in fact, than modern times. Nine types of marriage were also available, ranging from arranged marriages between social equals, a second wife and the right to visit a mistress regularly. Divorce was also an option, and a woman could turn to it if, among other things, her husband discussed her sexual performance publically, had used magic to trick her into marriage or was simply too fat for love-making.

The system would later become a justification for the Anglo-Norman invaders, who saw themselves as cleaning up the moral mess of the natives, their rules and their church. The Brehon laws, however, were to continue in some form until the early seventeenth century.

Before the Normans arrived, ringforts were still common settlements, as they had been for hundreds of years, but by the eleventh century many of the monasteries had largely outgrown their original, purely religious function, and formed a wider role in society, attracting people and a degree of urbanisation.

As well as farming, a certain amount of hunting was going on—enough to drive the wild boar to extinction in Ireland during the twelfth century. Seals were also hunted for skin and meat. The whale bones that have been found at some archaeological sites did not end up there as the result of hunting but were probably washed up on the shore. Such an arrival would have been treated as something of a gift by coastal dwellers. The bones would have been of value, as would the meat.

Dublin was still effectively a Scandinavian city. The kingships of Dublin and Leinster had become increasingly linked in the previous decades, enough that the King of Leinster needed to hold the Dublin title in order to be considered fully in control of his territory. The 'Ostmen' (so named because their territory was on the east coast) had their own king too, whose switching of allegiance would eventually hurt MacMurrough greatly.

The full story of the violent claims and counter-claims to the highkingship of Ireland is, frankly, complex.

Turlough O'Connor, King of Connacht and a man set on becoming high king, was a busy man during the early 1100s; dividing kingdoms, engaging in military campaigns, building a naval fleet on sea and garrisons on land. He created his own mint. He created an alliance with the King of Norway. He specifically built an infrastructure with the intention of speeding up his battle plans, including a canal between the River Suck and the River Shannon and also a wattle bridge over the Shannon at Athlone.

He built several *caislean,* or wooden castles, which acted as military outposts. That they were constructed of wood could be troublesome, as is seen by how one in Ballinasloe was destroyed by 'casual fire' in 1131. He placed a *caislean* on the east bank of the Shannon at Athlone to guard his new bridge, but it burned down in that same year after it was struck by lightning. Not wanting to let the problem get him down, Turlough ordered that the *caislean* be rebuilt. It was, only to be destroyed in 1133. He built it again. It lasted another two years. Many others would have given up, but his men had another go and this time the *caislean* lasted until 1155, when it was destroyed in a fight and its remains finally left to rot once and for all.

Turlough O'Connor's 50-year reign was a bloody one. He tried to carve up his rivals—going into Munster, briefly installing his son as King of Leinster and Dublin. The end result was a yo-yoing of power, in which his various military campaigns triggered counter-strikes by an alliance of enemies, with O'Connor's power at one point whittled back to Connacht before, through negotiations and battle, growing again.

By 1145, the Annals of the Four Masters tell us that Ireland was a 'trembling sod'. In 1151, there is mention of a great battle in Cork that is said to have killed 7,000 Munstermen. The Annals of Inisfallen also give a sense of just how dangerous things had become. Here are successive entries for 1165, four years before the arrival of the invaders:

1165.4: Conchobar Ua Diarmata was *slain*.

1165.5: Donnchad, son of Tadc, son of Domnall, was *blinded*.

1165.6: Gilla na Trínóite Ua Dálaig, ollav of Desmumu, was *slain*.

1165.7: A great hosting by Ruaidrí Ua Conchobuir and by Muirchertach, son of Tairdelbach, into Desmumu, and Gilla Ailbi Ua Dedaid was *slain* by them.

1165.8: Donnchad, son of Cinnétig Ua Cinn Fhaelad, was *slain*.

1165.9: Flaithbertach Ua Domnaill was *slain*.

1165.10: Senguala, with its church and many people, was *burned*.

The Church was constantly involved in negotiating peace deals and surrenders. Armies could be large, with a growing reliance on cavalry and, when necessary, ships. In 1137, Dermot MacMurrough's forces had combined with the King of Thomond's to gather 200 ships for a siege of Waterford.

Clearly, an outbreak of warfare would make life considerably more difficult than it already was. It seems that it wasn't uncommon for soldiers to billet in civilian households. Historians can deduce this in part because churches were often granted immunity from such billeting, as the arrival of soldiers was a drain on precious resources. The average life for an Irish male at the time involved some farming or labouring, depending on his profession, and a little fighting, depending on the attitude of his local king. While the chieftains wore helmets, carried shields, a lance or spear, a sword and armour, their foot soldiers would have wielded axes and slingshots. All freemen were expected to fight, although slaves didn't have to, allowing them at least one benefit from their otherwise misfortunate state. Women and clergy were also exempt.

Power was often asserted in a much more direct way, such as the relatively common practice of blinding an enemy or potential usurper by jabbing a needle into his eye. The enemy's disability would prohibit him from being chief or king.

Blinding was carried on for centuries, and was particularly rife in the years leading up to the Norman invasion. Blood ties were no protection from blinding. In fact, they were sometimes a positive disadvantage. There are many examples of brothers blinding brothers, fathers blinding sons. It was a merciless tactic that would have required nerves (and presumably several people) to carry out, and would have been terrifying for the victim. Nor was blinding the only tactic used. Castration was also an effective way of ensuring an end to a rival's dynastic ambitions.

Through O'Connor's reign his influence shifted, his allies and enemies changed, and the only constant was his ability to hang on to power regardless of who he had to kill, bribe or usurp in order to do so. It meant making enemies. Among them was the King of Leinster, Dermot MacMurrough, although the relationship vacillated between enmity and alliance, with O'Connor at one point invading and trying to usurp MacMurrough, but later giving him a slice of Meath as a sign of their supposed allegiance.

All of which would have been yet another sideshow in the ongoing power struggle on the island, if it wasn't that in 1152 MacMurrough kidnapped Dervogilla, the wife of a fellow called Tiernan O'Rourke, the one-eyed King of Breifne (a tract that mostly covers today's Leitrim). O'Rourke was a strong ally of Turlough O'Connor's. The consequences would turn out to be greater than anyone involved could ever have imagined.

MacMurrough nabbed Dervogilla from her home—taking some furniture and cattle into the bargain—before bolting. Dervogilla is described as having given a decent impression of someone who didn't want to be taken: screaming and kicking as she was carried from her home. Historians have long believed that she protested a little too much, because the two are generally assumed to have been illicit lovers. They were both middle-aged at the time, so it was not youthful folly. MacMurrough brought her to his place at Ferns, where she spent quite some time until her stay was brought to a sudden halt by the arrival of Turlough O'Connor, who grabbed her on behalf of her husband and returned her to him.

O'Rourke was not the forgiving type, and his revenge would have extraordinary consequences. Yes, Ireland would probably have been invaded by England at some point in time; and, yes, the complexities of the Irish rivalries had reached a climactic moment. Yet, among the main reasons why the Anglo-Normans invaded when they did, why Ireland began its 800 years-and-counting of occupation, is because of a bit of hanky-panky between people who really should have been old enough to know better.

Turlough O'Connor died in 1156, and the next high king was a chap called Muirchertach Mac Lochlainn. Clearly not the most diplomatic of sorts, he invited a rebellious king to his house as an Easter guest and took the opportunity to blind him. This was such a breach of etiquette that it ultimately convinced other kings to dethrone him. Turlough O'Connor's son, Rory, bought the loyalty of the Dublin Ostmen by giving them 4,000 cows, then he divided the north, attacked and killed Mac Lochlainn and took the high-kingship of Ireland.

When he took control of Dublin, Rory O'Connor was happy to allow MacMurrough a free hand in his kingdom in return for his loyalty. Tiernan O'Rourke, though, was in far less of a conciliatory mood. He took with him a troop of Ostmen from Dublin and marched towards MacMurrough's territory. The King of Leinster, experienced enough to know when the game is up, fled.

So it was that he came to be wandering England and France in search of a king, and that he found himself in 1167 reading Henry II's letter to anyone who would listen, and probably a few who weren't so inclined to. Eventually, he attracted the attention of one fellow who was somewhat down on his luck and looking for a chance to reclaim some glory and win some land. His name was Richard Fitz Gilbert de Clare. The Irish would come to know him better as Strongbow.

———

In Dublin's Christ Church Cathedral is what appears to be the simple but striking tomb of Strongbow, described by an accompanying plaque as 'fyrst: and: pryncypall: invader: of: Irland: 1169: Qui: Obiit: 1177'.

There are some small, but significant, details to note. He wasn't the first invader, although posterity has given him that honour. He died a year earlier than the plaque says. And the 'tomb' is only a monument, the original having been destroyed when part of the church collapsed on it in 1562. In fact, eight years later a replacement effigy was installed, and while his bones did not join it, it is possible that his internal organs were interred in whatever state they could be in 400 years after their owner had perished.

Finally, but worth noting, the likeness is not actually Strongbow's. It may be modelled on the Earl of Drogheda at the time.

Beside the tomb is a smaller effigy, representing his son. Through the centuries, its size has been explained as follows: so enraged was he by his son's cowardice in battle, Strongbow cut the boy in half. That it's not true (the boy died in childhood) doesn't stop it from being repeated in some books even now.

The other problem with Strongbow's reputation is the nickname. Because of it, you might presume that he had quite a reputation as an archer. Not at all. His nickname was a hand-me-down, inherited from his father, Gilbert, who was genuinely skilful with a bow. The Strongbow we know was a veteran of a few battles, but nothing that had earned him his moniker. (Although, he is now more familiar by that name, so we'll continue to use it here.)

When MacMurrough turned up looking for help, it really was a stroke of luck for Strongbow. He had become an increasingly marginalised figure in Wales. His title, Earl of Pembroke, had been taken from him, along with much of his estate, because he had sided with Stephen during the English civil war and hadn't transferred his loyalty to Henry II.

Strongbow was still powerful, with some land and a couple of small castles. But he was about 50 years old and a widower. Life was not treating him as kindly as he would have liked. Until, at least, Dermot MacMurrough showed up in south Wales looking for help.

Famously, Strongbow was offered MacMurrough's daughter, Aoife, as part of the deal. A couple of other Welsh-Norman half-brother barons, Robert fitz Stephen and Maurice fitz Gerald, were recruited with the promise that they would get Wexford. Fitz Stephen had only recently been a prisoner of a local nobleman, so MacMurrough's arrival proved quite an upswing in his fortunes too.

Strongbow may have been the leader of the invasion, but he was far from being the 'principal' invader as the Christ Church monument claims. In fact, Strongbow would eventually be one of the last of the first wave. It was MacMurrough who led the way, returning to Ireland with a handful of mercenaries in August 1167 and, with little difficulty, he took back his patrimonial kingdom of Ui Chennselaig (Kinsella), before facing up to an angry Rory O'Connor, and an even angrier Tiernan O'Rourke. So, MacMurrough submitted to the high king, and agreed to give some compensation to the one-eyed king. But he was not about to back down.

The moment when the Anglo-Normans actually landed in Ireland, and began a long, painful new era in the relationship between the two islands, came in May 1169 when Robert fitz Stephen and another knight, Maurice de Prendergast, arrived with a combined force of over 500 men.

They proceeded first to once more establish MacMurrough's dominance in Leinster. Then, they began to fight amongst themselves when de Prendergast defected to another king. Further forces arrived from Wales the following May, and joined a force that marched on Dublin and forced the Ostmen into submission.

So, it was at this point that MacMurrough sent letters to Strongbow suggesting that he get over to Ireland quick. Having been given the go-ahead by Henry II, Strongbow finally landed near Waterford on 23 August 1170. He had with him about 200 knights and 1,000 soldiers.

He went on to capture Waterford and then to get his promised bride, Aoife. He then headed towards Dublin and proceeded to take the city after surprising Rory O'Connor's forces at Castleknock.

However, his power in Ireland became something of a concern to Henry, who feared that Strongbow might decide to forcibly recover his lost earldom of Pembrokeshire. There was nothing for it but for Henry to bring his curved legs to Ireland to stamp his authority on affairs. Plus, he needed to duck out of England for a while to let things calm down following his role in the assassination of the Archbishop of Canterbury, Thomas Becket.

In October 1171, Henry landed at Waterford with 500 knights and 3,000 archers. It was such an impressive show of force that they managed to intimidate the Irish into submission. Henry's campaign in Ireland didn't involve a single pitched battle. Instead he spent six months harrying and ravaging the countryside in order to both stock up on supplies—vital for any extended campaign—and deny them to his enemy. In the course of this, a large number of Irish kings submitted to him (probably because he was considered the better of two evils) and the Irish bishops endorsed his invasion.

Strongbow, meanwhile, begged forgiveness for having become a little carried away and agreed to Henry's right to be overlord of Ireland.

The English king's invasion, then, had been something of a success, and he might have achieved more if some of his sons hadn't launched a rebellion in cahoots with the King of France.

Henry left Ireland in 1172. In that same year, Tiernan O'Rourke—he of the one eye and the errant wife—went to the Hill of Ward in Meath to talk with Hugh de Lacy, an Anglo-Norman baron. The meeting ended with O'Rourke's death. His body was strung up and his head sent to Henry.

None of which was of any solace to Dermot MacMurrough, because he had died the previous year.

For Rory O'Connor, the arrival of the neighbours from the east eventually forced him back into Connacht. Until then he had enjoyed the role of high king, going on a triumphant tour of the country, beginning work on a cathedral in his capital of Tuam, Co. Galway, and holding the Tailteann games, a sort of Irish Highland Games. It would be the last event of its kind until a rather ridiculous, expensive and doomed attempt to revive them by the newly independent Ireland in 1924.

Rory O'Connor proved to be the last uncontested High King of Ireland, eventually being deposed by his own son in 1186.

As for Strongbow, he had taken the title of Earl of Leinster once MacMurrough died and then went on a rampage in an attempt to secure the province for settlers from his estates back home. He died in 1176. His end was most ignoble and deeply unpleasant: he was killed by a gangrenous foot ulcer.

———

The annals, as they so often did, took a minimalist attitude to one of the most significant moments in the island's history. They are as perfunctory about this period as they are about all others, although, as you read them, just when you believe their compilers to have been allergic to all colour, you'll be ambushed by an entry like this in the Annals of Inisfallen from 1105: 'In the above year a camel, an animal of remarkable size, was brought from the king of Alba to Muirchertach Ua Briain.'

The recipient was the King of Dublin, a great-grandson of Brian Boru, so it must indeed have been some sight to see a possibly travel sick and disorientated camel being walked through the streets to his house.

1105 turned out to be quite a year for unusual animals, because the very next entry tells us that: 'In the same year there was caught by fishermen in the sea of Luimnech a fish of unheard of size, which measured fifteen feet.' It adds only that the fishermen earned two ingots of gold for their catch, although you have to believe that the tale was told in far more florid detail in the hostelries of Limerick.

The Annals of Ulster have this to say about the invasion force landing in the south-east of the country: 'The fleet of Robert Fitz Stephen came to Ireland in aid of Mac Murchadha.' It assumes you know the rest.

Here is the entry relating to Henry II's arrival in Ireland: 'The son of the Empress came to Ireland and landed at Port Láirge. The son of Cormac and the son of Tairdelbach submitted to him there, and he proceeded thence to Áth Cliath and remained there during the winter.'

Ultimately, the Irish account of the Norman invasion would rely on these perfunctory entries in the annals, as well as on the bardic poetry. The history that would come first to be accepted, and later to be questioned, came from Giraldus Cambrensis, Gerald of Wales.

Gerald was a priest whose grandmother had possessed great beauty and, it is claimed, a greater sexual appetite, which ensured that he was related to many of those who would eventually head the conquest of Ireland.

He wrote two books about Ireland, *Topographia Hibernica* (The Topography of Ireland) and then *Expugnatio Hibernica* (Conquest of Ireland). The latter included the first recorded—and long disputed—text of the supposed *Laudabiliter*. Gerald is hardly to be trusted in his account because members of his own family had led the invasion. He did not even join them on the original quest, arriving only later, plus, his accounts were not written until almost 20 years after the event, during which time his subjectivity had had ample time to swell.

However, his writings on Ireland are important for several reasons, including a role in popularising the now centuries-old stereotype of the Irish as lazy, backwards, treacherous sods. Gerald had—and still has—many fans, who consider his books to be important social histories. There are indeed some fascinating glimpses into life in Ireland at the time, but his portrayal would prove horribly problematic for the Irish for centuries afterwards.

Topographia Hibernica was split into three parts. The first looked at the landscape and wildlife of the land; the second the lives of its saints and the history of its miracles; but it is the third which most attracts the eye. Here, Giraldus wrote of the inhabitants—largely from his own encounters with them. A quick glance at the chapter index gives the reader a hint of what's ahead.

They include:

How the Irish are very ignorant of the rudiments of their faith.
Of their abominable treachery.
Of a new mode of making a league, a proof of their wickedness.
How they love their foster children and foster brothers and hate their own brothers and kindred.
How new comers are stained with the same vices.
Of a new and monstrous way of inaugurating their kings.

The Irish, he wrote, are 'so barbarous, they cannot be said to have any culture'. There is a chapter on 'the number of persons in this nation who have defects'. He comments, 'No wonder if among an adulterous and incestuous people, in which both births and marriages are illegitimate, a nation out of the pale of the laws, nature herself should be foully corrupted by perverse habits.'

Clearly, not all of his contemporaries were impressed with his yarns, because he used the preface of his second book, *Expugnatio Hibernica*, to defend himself against one critic who accused him of falsehoods in *Topographia Hibernica*. He stood firmly by his stories about talking wolves, a bearded woman, a creature with the head of a man and the 'extremities' of an ox, and a goat and a lion that had had intercourse with a woman.

Gerald's tone was in keeping with a general shift in English writing that began to openly describe the Scots, Welsh and Irish with contempt. The Welsh were a 'barbarous race' of 'untamed savagery'. The Scots were 'a barbarous nation' who can be insulted as 'worthless . . . with half-bare buttocks', a view which was firmly established after an invasion of the region in 1138.

These views had grown out of the disparity between the economy and society of the Anglo-Normans and those elsewhere on the islands. The Irish, like the native Welsh, were seen as morally corrupted, with their divorces and concubines. Their almost constant rivalries also contrasted with the relative peace in the Norman territories. 'The French ransom soldiers,' wrote Gerald, 'the Irish and Welsh butcher and decapitate them.'

So, the Irish mission was often treated as a civilising one—by Henry, by Rome, by the invaders—even if it was first carried out by those whose main motivation was materialistic. The writings of Gerald ensured that history was written by the winners, but it also provided the background to what the University College Dublin professor Terry Dolan has described as the 'political, cultural, linguistic and literary apartheid' practised by the settlers in Ireland.

What else, then, did the Anglo-Normans bring with them? Most obviously, they brought people, although we don't really know how many colonists came here, because there are no population statistics from medieval Ireland. Throughout the period, right up until the nineteenth century, in fact, Irish population figures were either absent or misleading. It was as late as the seventeenth century before an attempt was made to identify how many people lived on the island, and even then they were done only for taxation purposes and to assess available manpower for military purposes, so the results are unreliable.

However, Ireland would have been an attractive proposition for some at a time when England, and western Europe in general, was experiencing rising land and food prices as a result of over-population that would soon be curtailed by the Black Death. However, not as many found it as attractive as the English Crown would have liked. After Henry II came to Ireland, he allowed Rory O'Connor to continue to be high king of the unconquered parts of Ireland. There were some conditions, among them that O'Connor had to enforce a tax of every tenth saleable hide skinned in Ireland and had to insist that every native who had fled conquered land return and work it. All of this gives us the idea that the tenants were not yet flocking from England.

The Normans set about establishing nucleated towns, founding Kilkenny, Trim and many villages along the east of the island, and developing the Viking towns of New Ross and Drogheda. They fitted in, to a certain extent, by building their manor houses in areas already politically defined before their arrival.

These towns were planned in a way not seen before. The Vikings had developed their streets along natural contours, as can still be seen in the curving laneways of some of Ireland's cities today. The Anglo-Normans often planned their towns with a little more precision, being concerned with giving merchants street frontage and with setting up marketplaces. It meant that they brought labourers, stoneworkers, carpenters and others whose skills were required to develop the towns, although it's interesting to note from archaeological evidence that the standard of woodworking in Dublin's Wood Quay actually declined after their arrival.

However, their physical legacy is still around, in the castles and churches they built, such as St Patrick's Cathedral in Dublin, St Canice's in Kilkenny and the rebuilt Christ Church Cathedral in which Strongbow is buried.

The lords brought knights because the land in Norman Ireland was run on feudal lines: the tenant-in-chief rented out land to a fief who was required to provide at least one knight. This was because the tenant-in-chief was required to give the king, when he needed it, a specified number of armed, trained and mounted knights. The total rent for Meath was 50 knights. For Leinster it was 100. By 1216, the rent for all of Ireland was 427 knights.

Trade developed under the Anglo-Normans so that, by the thirteenth century, Ireland had become a major exporter of wool to England. Wine was a luxury, but because it was taxed heavily we have plenty of records of its popularity here. It came mostly from France, of course, and a little also came from Spain. It was re-exported to Scotland and England through Irish ports. Ireland also began to export horses.

The invaders attempted to replicate the English legal and political systems. They also introduced the jury system, began to install a county organisational system and brought in the idea of a state budget. The chief governor or lieutenant was the Crown's representative in Ireland, with much of his time spent travelling the country, accompanied by an armed guard, attempting to enforce English justice and collect revenues. The amount actually gained wasn't that impressive, a little more than £2,000 in 1360, and half of that by the fifteenth century.

The Anglo-Normans brought with them a version of parliament, although it was representative only of the colonists. From the off, there was a concern to separate the newcomers from the natives, culturally as well as politically. Among the first laws passed was one ordering that the settlers not wear Gaelic dress.

The word 'parliament' came from the French for 'discuss', and the legislation was usually written in that language too. This is a reminder that their arrival marked the invasion of two new languages, one of which would eventually supplant the native tongue. Before the Anglo-Norman invasion, the two languages of Ireland had been the Gaelic spoken by the ordinary people and Latin as used by the clergy. The Normans added English and the Norman-French that was then the language of their ruling classes.

French, as we have seen, was also the language of the English court and would remain the language of official written diplomacy there until as late as the early fifteenth century. In Ireland, while it became fashionable in literature, French quickly dissipated as a spoken language, although not before leaving behind several words in the Irish language, including *buidéal* ('botel'/'bottle') and *dinnéar* ('diner'/'dinner'). In the south of Ireland, a slang word for boy, *garsún*, is clearly influenced by the French word *garçon*.

This was not all the Anglo-Normans brought. Religious orders were introduced, such as the Dominicans, Augustinians, Carmelites and Franciscans. They brought rabbits, to join the native hare. And they also seem to have brought shoes. Lots of shoes. That we know so much about the footwear of medieval Ireland has much to do with how well leather—or animal hide— preserves. So we know that in the Dublin of the twelfth and thirteenth centuries, High Street was a cobbler quarter and throughout the city a visitor would have seen men wearing leather gloves and belts and sporting leather scabbards and purses. Not only did they wear leather, but they exported it in large numbers, mainly into north-west Europe. And recycling was common. If a large shoe was worn down, the upper part of it would be remade into a smaller shoe.

Bone combs were a prized and clearly practical commodity, often made out of antlers shed from deer. The Anglo-Normans, it seems, brought with them stronger bone and wood combs that replaced the intricate, but weak, smaller combs of the Viking era. They were plentiful. In the High Street and Christ Church areas alone 600 examples have been found. Goat and sheep horns were also useful for making trinkets.

———

As if the Irish didn't have enough problems with their own battling kings, the arrival of the invaders meant that they were now dragged into the regular wars of accession that went on in England. In 1487, a ten-year-old boy called Lambert Simnel was crowned King Edward VI in Christ Church Cathedral, with the full backing of noblemen led by the Earl of Kildare. An army was raised and headed to England to claim the throne, only to be defeated quickly. Simnel was pardoned and given a job as a kitchen boy.

Only four years later, a Perkin Warbeck—himself only a teenager—landed at Cork claiming a right to the English throne. Showing an impressive inability to learn from his mistakes, the Earl of Kildare refused to discount the possibility that he might indeed be heir to the throne. This so exasperated Henry VII, who had already pardoned him once, that the earl was arrested, brought to England and thrown into the Tower of London. Warbeck was hanged.

Yet, despite such tests of loyalty, the colonisers considered themselves English, rather than Norman or Anglo-Norman and certainly not Anglo-Irish. The idea that they became 'more Irish than the Irish themselves' can't actually be traced any further back than the seventeenth century.

In 1297, the Parliament did complain that some English had started dressing like the Irish and growing their hair in the native style (shaved on top, long at the back), something which had become enough of a problem that several Englishmen who adopted the style were killed through mistaken identity.

There was indeed growing cultural cross-fertilisation. Some of the colonists wore local dress and spoke Irish, but the Gaelic culture was also infiltrated by the customs, law and administrative practices of the English. Irish were brought into the settlers' society and fosterage between Irish and English families was not uncommon.

It was, of course, more complex than that. There was a marked separation between the cultures, the most obvious being the geographic boundary of the English Pale, a sphere of influence that stretched around Leinster, although it was prone to constriction depending on circumstances. That term seems to have first been used in 1495, when there was some discussion in the Parliament about digging ditches around it. Taking in Dublin, Kildare, Meath and Louth, it was the area which the English treated as the border between the bit of Ireland they had some control over and that which they most certainly did not.

By the way, the word itself is from the Latin *paleus*, meaning 'a stake', and developed to mean a row of stakes that formed a fence, before becoming a byword for boundary. And Calais, in northern France, had a Pale first, a mention of it the year before its Irish debut undoubtedly linked to the plans to develop a similar defensive boundary in Ireland. (The phrase 'beyond the pale' only took hold in the seventeenth century.)

And what of the Gaelic kings who were more literally beyond the Pale? For the next couple of centuries, some of the families continued to fight the invaders, as well as each other. In an effort to rid themselves of one foreign ruler, they even looked to other foreigners to come in and take over. In 1263, they offered to make the Norwegian king, Haakon IV, High King of Ireland, only for him to die before he had a chance to give it a go.

Before that, the last person to proclaim himself High King of Ireland had actually been a Scot, Edward Bruce (brother of Robert), who was invited in by the O'Neills of Ulster, but was opposed by other kings. He arrived in Ireland in 1315, and began three years of war until he was killed in battle and his body was quartered and distributed for public spectacle across Ireland. Except for his head, which was sent to the English king (although it has been speculated that they cut up the wrong body).

The fighting meant that there was a busy market for mercenaries, with bands of what were called 'kerns' roaming the country, hiring themselves out to whoever would pay for their services. They have been described as being 'barefooted, bare-headed and lightly-armed', yet they seem to have been in demand. And when they weren't, they often fell back on old-fashioned banditry to make their keep. There were similar bands of Anglo-Normans offering their services, so allegiances could be bought from both sides. When, in the fourteenth century, those ran dry, they were replaced by Scottish mercenaries. They were named galloglasses, a bastardised version of the Irish for 'foreign warriors'.

Among the common Irish there developed a belief that a messiah would return to free them from the invaders, itself an adaptation of similar prophecies that spread amongst the people during the early part of the Viking invasion. Stoked by the Bardic poets, the rumours were so strong that in 1214 one fellow was declared Aodh, the Deliverer; the one who had come to lead them to victory.

Despite such expressions of desperation, there were some advantages to being an Irish peasant. Most obvious was that they were still living away from towns, scattered through the country-side. This was to prove something of a blessing when the Black Death arrived in Ireland.

As the colonists went from being Anglo-Norman to being Anglo-Irish, it occurred against a background of famines caused by poor harvests and plagues. The Irish lived in a primarily rural setting, while the urbanised Anglo-Irish were far more susceptible to the whims of the market. Entire towns were abandoned.

Ireland was already familiar with disaster. War and climate had contributed to several famines in the decades approaching the outbreak of the plague. There had been a famine in 1294 that was so severe that people were said to have cannibalised bodies that had been hung from the gallows in Dublin.

There had been a severe famine between 1315 and 1318, which coincided with Edward Bruce's invasion. The hunger of his army was said to be so bad that they dug up corpses to feed on them. This may well be an invention, or mere exaggeration, but there is no doubt that pestilence and famine were relentless in Ireland at the time, adding only to the quite astounding number of gruesome diseases which already circulated: gonorrhoea, anthrax, leprosy, scabies, scurvy, dysentery and smallpox. If one germ didn't get you, there were plenty of others lining up to have a go. It's clear why the average lifespan of a European born between 1350 and 1500 was a mere 26 years of age; it's more surprising that this didn't vary depending on how wealthy a person was.

The colonisation had already lacked a cohesive plan, and settlers had been faced with not only the resilience of the population but the vagaries of geography. The drumlins, boglands, lakes and mountains of the border between the midlands and Ulster proved to be a particularly tough landscape. The Anglo-Normans themselves fought between each other, and gradually a combination of these power struggles, excessive taxes from the Crown and the conscription of men from Ireland to fight English wars in Scotland and Wales as well as the power struggles between the Anglo-Normans, led to a diminution of their influence and the resurgence of the Gaelic kings in large parts of Ireland. The Pale grew smaller.

But there was nothing that set the colonisers back more than the arrival of the Black Death in Ireland in 1348. The plague first entered the country somewhere along the east coast—Drogheda, Howth and Dalkey are all candidates—and spread quickly in each direction along the coast and inland. Meanwhile, it also arrived into Waterford port, and travelled up the River Nore to Kilkenny.

That it spread quickly must have had something to do with the particularly unhygienic conditions of the towns. If you'd like an idea of just how filthy a large Irish town would have been in 1348, and how receptive it was to the rats and fleas that carried and transmitted the plague, then read Maria Kelly's *The Great Dying: The Black Death in Dublin* and *A History of the Black Death in Ireland*, which describe it vividly. In Dublin, for instance, drains ran through the middle of the streets, occasionally running red with the blood of dead animals, and would have been rancid from waste. Pigs wandered the streets, because almost every house kept them.

In Kilkenny, the city authorities in 1337 had decreed that:

> If anyone be found washing clothing or the intestines of animals or anything else in the fountain of the said town they shall be forfeited and if anyone be found committing any other enormity in the said fountain he shall be put into the tumbrel.

A tumbrel was a type of ducking stool, on wheels, which tipped the person into the water. Whether it was sufficient to dissuade people from doing an 'enormity' in the fountain, we cannot know.

Although wealthier houses had their own toilets, which flowed directly into the nearest river, everyone else made do with either public toilets or the street. It's no coincidence, then, that 1300s thinking was that noxious smells were a cause of the disease.

By 1348, Dublin probably had a population of about 20,000 and our best account of the Black Death in the city is thanks to a Franciscan friar, John Clyn, who documented the devastation.

> Many died of boils and abscesses and pustules which erupted on their shins or under their armpits; others died frantic with pain in their head and others spitting blood ... this plague was at its height in Kilkenny during Lent; for on the sixth day of March eight of the Friars Preachers died. There was hardly a house in which only one had died, but as a rule man and wife with their children and all the family went the common way of death.

Clyn claimed that 14,000 died of the plague, a figure that is probably exaggerated, yet the worst outbreaks of the Black Death wiped out at least a quarter of the populations they affected in Europe, so it's likely that it was a similar figure in Dublin. Clyn was among its victims.

Its impact in Ireland was horrific. Before the plague, immigration had already slowed and areas had become depopulated. The sudden disappearance of perhaps a quarter of the population of the towns—and of similar numbers in England—led to obvious problems. The administration struggled to function effectively, labour shortages were a major problem and people stopped migrating to Ireland. The Black Death meant that construction work slowed to a trickle, and such was the shortage of people that even the church had to open up the priesthood to illegitimates for the first time. As an indication of the public mood, in September and October of 1348 a pilgrimage was organised at Teach Moling on the River Barrow, Co. Carlow, where thousands gathered—priests and common people alike—to wade in the waters and pray for deliverance.

The outbreak only exacerbated the problems that had been affecting the colony already. The plague would have impacted on the Gaelic parts of the island, but that it did so less than in the towns may be seen in how little it gets mentioned even in the traditionally pithy annals.

It was not the last outbreak, but only the most severe of many that visited the island for the next 300 years, and it formed a regular backdrop to the various problems that beset the country over those centuries. Chief among the invaders' problems was the task of trying to keep some order in a country which was mostly out of their control. Meanwhile, there developed an increasingly dysfunctional relationship between the Anglo-Irish and the English Crown to which they looked for help.

There were occasional attempts by English kings to sort out the Irish problem. But as the centuries progressed, a mutual suspicion developed as the Anglo-Irish believed that the Crown's indifference to, and absence from, Ireland was damaging. The Crown, meanwhile, came to view the Dublin administration as corrupt and the Anglo-Irish as being too close to the Irish.

In some respects, it was true. Although they did remain a class apart, many of the Anglo-Irish lords were slowly sucked into becoming, while not *more* Irish than the Irish, then a new breed of Irish. The names introduced at the time are now so engrained that they would hardly be seen as anything but native today. There were Fitzgeralds, Prendergasts, Fitzpatricks, Fitzsimons, Tobins, Redmonds, Butlers, Dillons and Tyrrells.

What would ultimately set the Anglo-Irish apart from the English was their religion. Their antecedents had come here in part to reform the Church, and when a far more explosive Reformation occurred, the fact that Ireland remained largely inured to its impact meant that the Catholic Old English were separated from the Protestant New English, and it was a distinction that would much later come to a head on the battlefield. By the time the Gaelic chieftains engaged in a pivotal rebellion against the English in the late sixteenth century—a rebellion that would lead to the Flight of the Earls and wholescale immigration through the Plantations—the Catholic Anglo-Irish lords were on the side of the Irish against the Protestant Crown.

They had become the Old English. But the era of the New English was dawning.

Chapter 5 ~

IF AT FIRST YOU DON'T SUCCEED… THE PLANTATIONS

During the 1550s, one writer rather giddily described Dublin as the 'young London'. It was nothing of the sort. It arguably matched London for squalor and disease, but not much else. It had little of the excitement and busy growth of its English counterpart. Instead, many of Dublin's most prominent buildings were in a semi-ruinous state. Dublin Castle, for example, was in such a perilous condition that government business was sometimes conducted in Christ Church Cathedral, although this venue proved itself to be no less reliable when a section of its roof and wall collapsed in 1562, crushing Strongbow's original tomb.

Nearby was the Tholsel, a merchants' hall, where people could find the Chain Book, containing the laws of the city and lists of prisoners in the city's jail. It earned its name because it was chained to the wall in an effort to prevent its theft—a successful tactic because it is today in safekeeping in Dublin's City Hall. Impressively, the Tholsel was also the site of the country's first mechanical clock, although by the 1600s this building would also be falling into ruin.

Fire was a constant problem in the city. If a person managed to put their fire out without it being seen from the street, then their relief would soon be tempered by a small fine. If the fire could be seen from the outside, then that fine could be doubled. In 1546, the council made an attempt to deal with the threat fire posed when it agreed that '12 graps of iron shall be made for pulling down houses that shall chance to be afire, 40 buckets of leather for carrying of water'.

By the turn of the century only one bridge spanned the Liffey, although buildings had begun to spread east beyond the city walls, with Trinity College founded on the site of a former monastery in 1592.

Dublin was joined only by Galway in having significant suburbs, but although its population was bolstered by refugees from wars and famines, who clustered in shanties on its fringes, by the late 1500s its inhabitants numbered at most only 10,000–15,000. It meant that the city couldn't afford catastrophes such as that of 1597 in which gunpowder exploded as it was being unloaded on the quayside, killing 126 people and injuring many more. The explosion levelled between 20 and 40 houses in the area of Merchant's Quay, Wood Quay and Winetavern Street and damaged many more houses and churches in the vicinity. It also destroyed the Customs House and the city's only crane. Dutch engineers had to be imported to build a new cranehouse. Even for a city well used to regular plague epidemics, this was a shocking loss of life and it had a big psychological impact on the residents.

Plague was still a recurring problem in Dublin, as it was across the country. It was believed that the disease was somehow carried by noxious air, stoked by the foul odours that would have filled the city's streets, and Dublin had enacted increasingly rigorous measures to halt epidemics. Only people coming from plague-free areas were allowed to enter the city and anyone wanting to leave was required to have a licence from the mayor. Residents of houses in which plague broke out were ordered to inform the authorities within 24 hours or be jailed for 80 days and then banished from the city. A pesthouse was established outside the city at George's Lane (later renamed George's Street), where four men were employed to look after the place. Their responsibilities included preventing delirious patients from running into the streets and panicking citizens, and they were paid 6d a day for the work. It must have been decent money, providing they lived long enough to spend it.

There was a terrible outbreak of plague in 1574, lasting from the summer until the end of October, when the cold weather seems to have dampened its virulence, only for it to recur again the following spring and spread throughout the Pale. One annalist wrote: 'This malady raged violently among the Irish and English in Dublin, in Naas of Leinster, Ardee, Mullingar, and Athboy. Between those places many a castle was left without a guard, many a flock without a shepherd, and many a noble corpse without burial, in consequence of this distemper.'

This epidemic was a massive inconvenience to Dublin, not least because many of its officials and wealthier residents upped and left the city. So many deserted, in fact, that they were ordered either to return by 1 July, or at least to send a deputy to discharge their duties on their behalf. Otherwise their citizenship would be revoked.

As a port, Dublin during the 1500s wasn't even the most effective on the island. A sandbar at the mouth of its bay made the wharves and loading docks inaccessible to large vessels, comparing badly to Limerick, for instance, which could accommodate 400-tonne ships and was described by one writer in the 1530s as being a 'wondrous proper city and strong . . . it may be called little London for the situation and plenty'.

Around Dublin, the Pale had shrunk under the combined forces of depopulation and warfare, and the administration staved off attacks by paying a 'black rent', so feeding a lucrative protection racket being run by the Gaelic lords. Ironically, among the families gaining from this arrangement was the MacMurroughs, the descendants of Dermot MacMurrough, who still controlled a large part of Leinster several centuries after their ancestor had invited the invaders in the first place.

Outside of the Pale, the English lived principally in protected settlements, although they were not nearly as protected as they would have liked, because they were constantly under threat of attack. In Co. Wicklow, there were the O'Byrnes and O'Tooles, who harried Dublin and raided Kildare, where there was also a rogue branch of Anglo-Irish, the 'Bastard Geraldines', who formed armed gangs and caused occasional mayhem.

For all that they terrified the colonists, the Irish armies were not always terribly efficient. The richer men would be on horseback, but while guns came into increasing use, many rode without stirrups and with their javelins raised over their heads. Going full steam ahead into battle, then, would have been a risky endeavour, because they were likely to meet English horsemen with heavy lances, stirrups and saddles.

But guerrilla campaigns were the preferred tactic and often brought terror to the settlers, while the English-led administration lived with the near-constant threat of rebellion and an accompanying dread that the Spanish would land on Irish shores to assist any such uprising. Such fears were entirely justified, because throughout the sixteenth century there were several rebellions, one of which—the Nine Years War—did eventually lead to a Spanish fleet landing at Kinsale.

In the rest of the country, the urbanisation of Ireland just hadn't happened. There were only two true towns in Connacht (Athenry and Galway) and just the one in Ulster (Carrickfergus). Disease was rife; one outbreak reportedly took a substantial part of the population of Cork, although it is also described as being little more than a long street at the time. Smallpox and typhus joined the plague in being regular killers.

War and disease led to depopulation, so that land was wasted and abandoned, with some monastic settlements falling into ruin. Most Irish lived in scattered settlements, some tilling land for two or three years before moving on elsewhere (although they did not yet have the potato as a crop or in their diet as it only arrived in

Ireland, probably from Spanish ships, in 1580). Because their houses were often made of clay and straw, they could be put up quickly and abandoned easily. Living standards were modest even among some of the native noblemen who, one English observer later mocked, lived in 'a poor house of clay, or a cabin made of boughs and trees and covered with earth, for such are the dwellings of the very lords among them'.

To the south-east of the island the major ports were Wexford and, more vital, Waterford, from where Ireland's hides and cloth went out including, between 1558 and 1589, a total of 961 wolf skins that were exported to Bristol. (The wolf was still relatively common at the time; the last one is recorded to have been killed by an unsympathetic farmer in Co. Carlow in 1786.)

The sailors of Waterford would have been regular visitors to France, Spain and Portugal, and its fishermen may have travelled as far as the fishing grounds off Newfoundland. Once they left the relative safety of the harbour, however, ships sailed into water that so teemed with pirates it had created a thriving black economy.

Although this was the era of the famous female pirate Grace O'Malley, women were more likely to be at the seedier end of the industry. Prostitution was rife in the ports, as made clear by the council of Munster when it griped not only of the number of men joining pirate ships, but of the 'shameless and adulterus women as daylie repaired unto them' in the local taverns of coastal villages such as Baltimore.

It made Ireland hugely attractive to pirates. Among them—for a time at least—was a Henry Mainwaring, an Oxford graduate who took to piracy before becoming such a successful pirate-hunter that he was knighted for his work. In his spare time, he also wrote a book, *Of the Beginnings, Practices and Suppression of Pirates*, in which he described Ireland as the 'nursery and store-house of pirates', in part because of its bays and harbours but also because of 'the good store of English, Scottish, and Irish wenches' who awaited them there.

Despite the many problems the English found themselves dealing with in Ireland, the Irish bardic poets were regularly concerned with the decline of the Gaelic lordships (even if many were relatively strong at this point) and the adoption of English fashions.

Retiring to a darkened room to compose a poem, the poet would commit it to memory and only write it down once he had emerged. He would then give the poem to someone else whose job was to learn it and recite it from memory. The performer was usually accompanied by a harp and would, undoubtedly, have added a certain drama to the pieces, especially those disapproving satires which made ready use of an exclamatory 'O' and occasional 'alas'.

Here is an example of one poet getting sniffy about how the English styles were affecting the Irish youth.

O man who follows English ways,
who cut your thick-clustering hair,
graceful hand of my choice,
you are not Donnchadh's good son!

You think the yellow head of hair unfashionable,
he detests both wearing locks
and going bald after the English style;
your characters are different indeed.

He would hate to carry at his ankle
a jewelled spur on a boot,
or stockings in the English style;
he will have no locks upon him.

Proving that certain complaints never age, another bard observed that the Irish were becoming less interested in religion, that women were losing the run of themselves and that drinking was ruining the country.

In her is no love of feast-days, no,
nor no recourse to the clergy:
the mirth of her bardic companies is no more,
the modesty of her maids is no more.

Alas for the ruin of the youths,
a noble-handed troop of valorous feats:
hard drinking subdues their sense,
that is the characteristic of all.

All in all, then, between the wars, the diseases and the cultural paranoia, Ireland was not the most attractive spot on earth for any prospective migrant. Which means that for a large-scale migration to have actually happened during the 1600s, tens of thousands of newcomers must have been keen to leave behind a particularly miserable spot. That place was Scotland.

———

The English—Old and New—made attempt after attempt to subdue and colonise Ireland and, for a people so doggedly certain about their supposed superiority, they struggled terribly to actually achieve it.

In the early 1500s, the ideas of what to do with Ireland were often chilling. It was suggested that the native Irish simply be forced off the land and replaced with a 'more docile' population. It wasn't the thought of genocide that caused a rethink, but that it wasn't logistically possible either to carry it out or to replace the population with enough settlers.

Gradually, the idea of plantation increasingly came to replace that of military conquest. Soldiers—garrisons of them—were expensive to keep. It was better to have citizen soldiers, working the land but armed against attack. It was supposed to be the answer to a few problems. It was seen as a chance to extend English control, civilise the Irish (or at least bulk up the civilised population) and turn a tidy profit at the same time.

The plantations of Ireland involved various large- and small-scale operations. Some were free enterprises and others were encouraged, or mandated, by the English Crown. And they needed repeated attempts until eventually, following Oliver Cromwell's defeat of the Irish Catholic rebellion in the mid-1600s, there was a settlement of English and Scots in Ireland that was not only big, but involved uprooting and transplanting a massive amount of Catholic Irish to do it.

It had all been kicked off in the 1500s by the first English King of Ireland, Henry VIII (his predecessors had only held the title Lord of Ireland), when he had tried a 'surrender and regrant' scheme which encouraged Gaelic lords to give up their lands with the promise of getting them back if they made themselves loyal only to the Crown. A more direct tactic developed with the various plantations of English that were then attempted, such as that in the 1550s in Laois which saw the county originally named the Queen's County after Mary, who was then monarch.

Actually, many of those who moved to Ireland during the 1500s did not come out of choice, but as soldiers pressed into the ongoing wars in Ireland. As the English made repeated attempts to impose themselves in various parts of the country, they weren't helped by the corruption of some officers, and the disinterest of many of their soldiers. It wasn't unusual, for instance, for some of those who came from England to sell their weapons to the enemy and use the proceeds to scarper.

Those soldiers who stayed were as likely to fall victim to illness as they were to the enemy. Dysentery, which killed many, was often referred to as 'the disease of Ireland', although it was also called by its more evocative name, 'bloody flux'.

It's worth pausing to imagine just how terrible the experience would have been for the soldiers in an age of few medicines, not to mention how undignified it would have been in an age of rudimentary, and sometimes non-existent, toilet facilities. Given the growing belief that the good Lord was on their side, there were times when their suffering appeared to be something of a cosmic joke, such as in 1521 when the English forces on the island suffered not just an outbreak of plague but a simultaneous bout of dysentery.

Politically, alliances were also messy, with some of the Old English now Gaelicised and standing alongside the Gaelic lords; some of the Gaelic lords fighting alongside, or even within, the English forces; and the English themselves so suspicious of everyone that only settlers who had been born in England were allowed positions within the administration.

As ever, the English were terribly concerned about their own people going native, although the reign of Henry VIII, and the establishment of the Church of England, had introduced religious divisions between the Old and New English that pushed their grievances beyond mere disgruntlement at their political circumstances.

In the latter half of the 1500s, Queen Elizabeth I made several attempts during her long reign to establish English settlements in Ireland. There were government-sponsored ventures, and there were private ones. Some of them were almost successful. Others were wholly disastrous.

One of the most notable examples is that of Sir Thomas Smith and his son (also Thomas) who, in 1571, were given a grant to lands that occupied a vast area of Ulster, stretching from Belfast Lough around Lough Neagh. There was one caveat: the land was already that of the O'Neills of Clandeboye. This would prove to be an important detail.

Smith was an interesting character. Giddy with notions of 'humanism', which thrived on the idea of civilising the barbarous, he was also a mover behind the Vagrancy Act of 1547, a law that forced into slavery any able-bodied poor who refused to work. (In fact, the Act was never enforced and was rapidly repealed.)

At his Essex home, Smith and his son would host debates on how Ireland would be best colonised. Should it be through gradually and peacefully building successful settlements? Or would it be just easier to go over there and kill whoever needed to be killed? Thomas Jr lobbied for the bloodier option; father favoured the softly-softly approach.

To promote their colonial project, they produced literature which explained that, 'Ireland lacketh only inhabitants, manurance and pollicie.' Having explained all the profitable advantages of relocating to this fine part of the world, the pamphlet concluded: 'How say you now have I not set forth to you another Eutopia?'

Naturally, the reality of Smith's Irish venture proved anything but Utopian. He saw this as an enterprise that could seek inspiration from the Romans, and eventually sent his son to Ireland having given him the rather grand advice to 'Mark Rome, Carthage, Venice, and all other where notable beginning hath been.' So, Thomas Jr went ahead, but in 1572 he landed at Strangford Lough with a miserably small party of only 100 people. The plan was to force out the local lords, but keep many of the lower classes to work in creating the settlement. It failed utterly. Within a year, Thomas Jr was dead, killed by his own Irish servants who were not as infused with the grandeur of this adventure as their employers. The rest of the party was eventually forced out by a native lord, Brian MacPhelim O'Neill, and by the time 1574 came around Sir Thomas Smith had lost a son, a slice of Ulster and any hope of making a fortune.

Other attempts at colonisation were far bloodier, if equally unsuccessful. Around Carrickfergus, Co. Antrim, Walter Devereux, the Earl of Essex and Governor of Ulster, planned to bring in 1,200 soldiers, the cost of which would be split between himself and Queen Elizabeth I. He planned to forcibly take the land he had been given—roughly the area of modern Antrim— but assured the queen that violence would be kept to a minimum, or at least to no more than 'the necessity of the cause requireth'.

Given how things actually turned out, it makes one shiver at quite how it would have been if he had been truly reckless.

Devereux turned out to have a flair for duplicity matched only by his bloodlust. In October 1574, he entertained Brian MacPhelim O'Neill, his wife and followers in a feast that was supposed to be aimed at reconciliation. It was a trap. Devereux ordered MacPhelim's arrest and the massacre of 200 of his clan. MacPhelim, his wife and brothers were taken to Dublin under the promise of a fair trial, but quickly executed.

Devereux next turned his attention towards a Scots community already living in the region. These were the followers of Sorley Boy McDonnell, the Irish-born son of a Scottish lord who had taken himself and his followers to the Antrim coast in the early 1500s after falling on the wrong side of a power struggle. Since then, the McDonnells had been a regular source of annoyance to the English, who worried that they might attract an invasion from Scotland.

Devereux argued that the Scots should be expelled and the Irish should no longer be allowed to 'nurse' on English wealth. He complained that English monarchs had too long given the Irish 'peaces, protections, pardons' instead of the 'sworde'. And when he became increasingly irritated by the queen's reluctance to lend him a hand ('Why should I wear out my youth in an obscure place without assurance of your good opinion?'), he then turned that sword towards the Scots.

In 1575, frustrated by Sorley Boy's apparent refusal to come out and fight openly, Devereux ordered an attack on Rathlin Island, where the wives and children of the soldiers had sought refuge, defended only by a small force of Scottish soldiers.

Led by two men (one of them a young Francis Drake) who had only just been introduced to each other, 200 soldiers set out for Rathlin on the morning of 22 July. Surprising the islanders, they chased them into a small castle, which was then battered by a couple of cannon rounds and a direct assault until the Scottish sent a constable out to discuss terms.

A long discussion followed, after which it was agreed to grant the constable, his wife and children safe passage off the island, but other requests to save certain people and goods were refused. Eventually, a deal of sorts was reached, encouraging the Scottish garrison to emerge from the castle. When they did, they were immediately set upon by the English soldiers—200 of the Scots were massacred almost immediately.

The rest of the island's population fled, taking refuge on cliffs and in caves. The next morning, as daylight crept over the island, Devereux's men hunted them down, rooted them out and killed them on the spot. By the end of the day, 300 men, women and children were dead. None were spared. Five days later, Devereux described it all in a letter to Elizabeth, boasting that this had been achieved with the death of only two of his own men.

If there is any meagre pleasure we can have from Devereux's life, it is in the manner of his death. His brutal adventures ultimately bankrupted him, and also helped to persuade Elizabeth that the Plantations were a blood-soaked folly that couldn't go on any longer. Following a visit to England, Devereux, bitter and angry, returned to Dublin, where he died of dysentery the following year. He was 36.

As for Sorley Boy, his answer to the massacre at Rathlin Island was to regain some of the land he had lost during previous battles against the English. After that, his most memorable contribution to the history books was a rather cryptic remark to the English, upon being shown his son's severed head nailed over the gate at Dublin Castle: 'My son hath many heads.'

War, then, was almost constant, and it was an era in which butchery was commonplace, and carried out by all sides, in which age or gender offered little protection. There was a saying at the time, in regards to the killing of children, that 'nits makes lice'.

The annals occasionally go into some detail on all of this, such as during the Desmond Rebellions in Munster—the first in 1569, the second 10 years later—which were led by an Old English family, the Fitzgeralds. The Annals of the Four Masters describe some of the atrocities supposed to have been perpetrated by the Earl of Ormond, an Anglo-Irish earl who led the attempt to quell the uprising, and the reprisals that followed.

> It was not wonderful that they should kill men fit for action, but they killed blind and feeble men, women, boys, and girls, sick persons, idiots, and old people. They carried their cattle and other property to the Lord Justice's camp; but great numbers of the English were slain by the plundered parties, who followed in pursuit of the preys . . . The Earl of Ormond also marched from Cork to Kerry, to join the Lord Justice. On this occasion they lost a countless number of men and horses, without bloodshed or slaughter, by the length of their march and journey, and a scarcity of provisions.

The annals may have exaggerated events, but there is no doubt that in Connacht and Munster at the time there were atrocious crimes against humanity. Beheading was a regular tactic: a common way for assassins to prove that a target was dead and for the wider public to see the evidence. It was also an insult, because headless bodies were denied a true burial. Instead, severed heads became increasingly more familiar sights on pikes in towns around the country.

According to the historian David Edwards, a beheading might be meted out for even relatively minor crimes, such as cattle-stealing, and once removed from its owner's shoulders the head would be stuck on a pole and displayed from a town wall as a warning to anyone else thinking of any banditry or rebelliousness.

Beheading often happened on a mass scale. In Munster, the queen's representative, a particularly vicious character called Humphrey Gilbert, led a campaign during which it was said he terrorised people by lining a path to his tent with the heads of their 'fathers, brothers, children, kinsfolk and friends', which—if true—was no doubt a grisly and effective method of gaining the upper hand in any negotiations.

The Munster plantations were triggered by the grabbing of land from the defeated Earl of Desmond and his allies, and they did show promise for a while. In 1588, there were about 3,000 settlers, but by 1598 that was up to 12,000. At times, though, the approach was hopelessly chaotic. A combination of logistics and human nature proved rather troublesome. For instance, there was such a gap between grants being given and people settling that by the time they actually arrived many of the Irish had reoccupied the land, either through the law or simply by squatting.

There were cases in which even the best-connected people would get their plot, rustle up the settlers and then head off for Ireland only to get there and find that the land they had been promised was already legally held by others. Court cases, as you might imagine, were a feature of the Plantations.

Even once they'd arrived in Ireland and claimed their land, settlers did not always settle, often quickly deciding to move somewhere more preferable. This added to the general movement of people across the Irish landscape. English soldiers were constantly on the march, as were the enemy armies and mercenaries. The Irish farmers were relatively nomadic, often moving with their cattle during the summer, a practice (booleying) the English looked down upon because they believed it helped to hide miscreants as well as stolen cattle, and that it also promoted laziness.

It was a tumultuous period in Irish history, in which wars and rebellions punctuated the decades, and we can only brush on the details here. In a nutshell, the Munster plantations ended when an Ulster rebellion in 1594, led by the O'Neills and O'Donnells, resulted in the devastating Nine Years War across the island and ultimately to a Spanish fleet landing in Kinsale, Co. Cork, failing to break out of there and contributing only to what would prove to be a pivotal defeat for the Irish. That war's arrival in Munster drove settlers off the land and towards Dublin or back to England and by the end of the sixteenth century, many of the Anglo-Irish earls were on the side of the Gaelic chiefs, now that they were linked by a common religion.

So, for a people who had repeatedly failed to stamp their authority on Ireland, the English really did have an exalted sense of their own greatness—and of the backwardness of the Irish— despite their repeated failures to subdue the island. The civilising zeal that underpinned the attitude of the English, Protestant Crown is considered by modern historians to be best summed up by the work of Edmund Spenser, an English settler, member of the administration in Ireland and author of the epic poem *The Fairie Queene.*

Born in 1552, Spenser was a Londoner and it is thought that his first poems were published when he was just a schoolboy. Although he was a sickly young man during his years at Cambridge, his poetry was greeted with great enthusiasm. He also went on to prove himself to be an impressive social climber and by 1580 he had been appointed secretary in the Dublin administration. In Ireland, he became something of a property whiz, before eventually coming into possession of Kilcolman Castle in Cork, where he engaged in various law suits against Catholic neighbours until he was burned out by the natives in 1598.

Spenser wound up in London, penniless and hungry. The writer Ben Jonson later claimed that, on hearing of Spenser's poverty, he sent him '20 pieces' only for the poet to return them with a note saying that he had no time to spend the money. Spenser died in 1599.

So, his time in Ireland was not a particularly happy one and there might have been considerable frustration poured into *A View of the Present State of Ireland*, a book probably written in 1596, but which was not actually published until 1633.

In the book, Spenser used the discussion between two bards to tease out his theories of the Irish race. The Irish and the Scots, he explained, could both trace their roots back to the Scythians, a nomadic race from Eurasia and prototypical barbarians. He used Irish haircuts and a supposed penchant for drinking blood as some of the proofs of this.

And the solution to taming these descendants of barbarians was simple and without great subtlety: 'the sworde'. The English had been too gentle before, was his argument. They must not make the same mistake twice. There must be 'no remorse or drawing back for the sight of any such rueful object as must thereupon follow, nor for compassion of their calamities'. Sure there could be more gradual approaches, using law and education and the introduction of planned colonisation, but without the threat of violence it would come to nothing. So, Spenser's plan was this: bring in 10,000 foot soldiers and 1,000 horsemen and tell the Irish that they had 20 days to comply with English demands. If they refused, then they should be hunted down and killed in winter when the cover is thin.

'If they be well followed one winter, ye shall have little work to do with them the next summer,' the book explained, as if discussing some farmland chore. And after all of that, and if there were any rebellious Irish left, famine would finish them off.

It might have taken Spenser's work over 30 years to finally reach a wider readership, but it was published against a background of growing religious zeal; a belief that Divine Providence was behind this mission. Spenser's attitude was not in any way unique, and the English elite's belief that the Irish were wild, barbarous and uncivilised often surfaced. In the account of one writer, Fynes Moryson, of his travels in Ireland, he claimed that 'some Irish (who will be beleeved as men of credit) report of Men in these parts yeerely turned into Wolves'.

Spenser had argued not just for the suppression of Gaelic culture but also for the reform of the 'degenerated' Old English, a process which would see them treated with as much ruthlessness as was shown to the Irish. The failures of the settlers were seen not as proof that the English Crown needed to put more effort into securing their areas, but as confirmation that they were generally useless.

As the sixteenth century dawned, Ireland was ravaged by a war that had cost a great deal of lives and money. It was not an attractive place to venture into. Yet, it was now that the Ulster plantations began in earnest.

They were triggered by the Flight of the Earls in 1607, during which the main chieftains of Ulster, having survived the end of the Nine Years War with their heads still on their shoulders, decided that their luck might be running out and fled to the Continent in the futile hope of returning with an invasion force. They never came back.

Instead, the great tracts of abandoned land were identified as ripe for colonisation. And it was a Scottish king who took up the challenge. James I had succeeded Elizabeth to the English throne in 1604, having already been James VI of Scotland since the age of one. It was James who the conspiracists had tried to blow up in the Gunpowder Plot of 1605. He was also highly unpopular with his own Parliament, who weren't altogether won over by his belief in the divine right of kings. It was he who commissioned the King James Bible, one of the most important books ever printed. And it was under him that the colonisation of North America began. The first permanent English colony, after all, was named Jamestown.

So, while he had no doubts about his own superiority, James also demonstrated how the English were not alone in believing themselves to be superior to the Gaels. He subscribed to the idea that there was a stark division between Gaelic and non-Gaelic peoples, especially in the islands off the west coast of Scotland. As a Scottish king, he was also involved in a similar 'civilising' programme, in which he planned to extend his power over the Gaelic populations of the Scottish Highlands. The colonisation of Ulster was suddenly an extension of this. Ireland, it was believed, needed social structures, a central government and stable land ownership. But more than this, it needed a new race: no longer Scots or English, but British.

The Ulster Plantations—in which six counties (Tyrone, Donegal, Armagh, Cavan, Fermanagh and the now defunct Coleraine) were to be filled with settlers—were to act as a buffer zone between the Irish and the Scottish Gaels. James himself explained that the people there had a tendency to break out in rebellion 'partly through their barbaritie, and want of civilitie, and partly through their corruption in Religion'.

The entire area of these six counties—not just the land pre-viously owned by the departed chiefs—was to be portioned out among three categories of landowners: so-called 'undertakers' in England and Scotland, who would get land that no Irish or Catholic could rent; English officials or soldiers; and finally the Church of Ireland, Trinity College Dublin and the king's representative, the Lord Deputy of Ireland, who were given about a quarter of the land available.

The undertakers were expected to bring at least 20 families, including 48 adult, English-speaking, Protestant males, from their own English or Scottish estates, to the 3,000 acres of Irish land that they would each be given.

Some of the schemes proved quite successful, even if the methods were unconventional. A couple of Scottish lords, Hugh Montgomery and James Hamilton, had agreed to go into business with a Gaelic chief from Co. Down, Con O'Neill, having first sprung him from jail thanks to a coiled rope rumoured to have been smuggled to him in a hollowed out cheese. By 1606, with O'Neill having sold his share of land in Down and Antrim, the Scots began attracting settlers in decent numbers to the area.

Not every region was so easily subdued. One that proved rather unattractive to settlers was an area that had traditionally been called 'O'Cahan's Country' (after its native chief) but which had latterly been renamed the County of Coleraine. This would become the only original Irish county to disappear before the twentieth century (the last Irish county created was Wicklow in 1606) and its extinction was caused by the arrival of County Londonderry, a place built on high ideals, low tactics and shaky foundations.

When the Crown realised that the Coleraine area of Ulster, at the centre of this particularly rebellious corner of the island, would be a costly and dangerous place to put a plantation, it decided to turn to the City of London. At this time, there were 12 Great Companies of the City of London, representing the Drapers, Fishmongers, Vintners, Goldsmiths, Merchant Tailors, Grocers, Mercers (textile dealers), Haberdashers, Salters, Ironmongers, Clothworkers and Skinners. These would be invited to finance the venture.

Not surprisingly, the Companies really weren't that keen on the idea. So, when they proved reluctant, the Crown's invitation became a not-so-subtle demand. Several of the City's leading figures were jailed or fined until they finally got the message that this was one project they would be involved in whether they liked it or not.

It caused some dismay to the City of London that it was being compelled to support the colonisation of a dangerous region, utterly lacking infrastructure. A fact-finding tour was organised in order to soothe their concerns, but it was carefully managed. The City of London's representatives were lodged in attractive houses, in the nicer parts of the province, and avoided the more dangerous parts altogether. Several English surveyors had recently been killed by Irish who didn't want their lands to be identified and then confiscated, so the tour itinerary avoided coming across any of those surveyors who had to do their work while under armed guard.

The Companies were not easily duped, and asked that their portion of the lands be expanded for the sake of security. They asked for territory to the east of the Bann (Coleraine, west Derry) and a nearby forest to source their timber. They got it all, and a whole new county named after them. This is how the area became known as Co. Londonderry, although the use of the 'London' part of the name is contentious even today—often to the point of daftness. At least one modern book settled for the ingenious, but clumsy, compromise of '(London)Derry'.

The planters were to create 12 estates, each going to one of the Companies. Because it was such an expensive business, some of the Companies had 'associates' attached to them in order to raise the levies needed to pursue it. For example, the Ironmongers brought with them the Brewers, Pewterers, Barber-Surgeons, Carpenters, Coopers, and Scriveners (representing London's scribes). So one might imagine that their corner of Ulster might be a good place if you wanted a beer, a haircut and someone to write down the adventures it all led to.

In all, 55 Livery Companies of the City of London—including Basket Makers, Musicians and Plumbers—were obliged to get involved in this costly undertaking. Each estate was to have a fortified manor house or 'castle', planned villages of houses of the 'English' type and a church. Collectively, they had to found and fortify two towns, Londonderry and Coleraine. They could at least set up their own courts. But it was all to be filled with English settlers, adhering to English law, speech, customs and the Protestant religion.

As the architectural historian Professor James Stevens Curl has pointed out, this idea was 'similar to the governing bodies of other seventeenth century joint-stock companies established for purposes of trade and colonisation'. They were private companies given the run of a frontier society. Londonderry was effectively to be a privately run county.

There were problems from the start. Most notably, the Irish method of measuring land was based not on its size but on its sustainability, so that the Companies ended up with far more land than they had planned for, and not all of it particularly good.

Settlements were half-built and, while there were supposed to be enough Londoners to surround and outnumber the natives, there were never sufficient immigrants to enable the Irish residents to be replaced and removed. So the security of the venture was always rather shaky and the settlers often went into illegal arrangements with the native Irish as a result.

With the accession of Charles I to the throne in 1625, the Crown showed little sympathy for any of these problems and instead found new ways to get money from the City of London, such as asking for finance for seven warships to help fight ongoing wars against France and Spain.

Eventually the City was brought to court, charged with violating the Articles of Agreement. It lost the case, was fined an enormous sum and its lands were confiscated. The landowners' titles were suddenly void and, to add to their general misery, they were also being charged enormous rents by the Crown. Some respite came in 1641 when the English House of Commons reversed the legal decision on the basis that the City had been treated wrongfully and should have the lands back. But it came a little too late. By then, the Irish had rebelled and destroyed every settlement other than Coleraine and Londonderry.

And in a way, the project would do for Charles I too. His arguments with Parliament over the region contributed heavily to the triggering of the English Civil War, and his eventually losing his head.

On a more practical level, travelling from London to the west of Ulster was not straightforward. A settler could take a full month to reach his destination, which was as long as it was then taking people to travel to the north American colony of Virginia. And when he arrived, the superiority of the British settlers in Ireland was not clear-cut.

For instance, although the British settlers built larger, more spacious households than the Irish farmers would have been used to, they were of inferior quality. Just as the Anglo-Norman settlers had arrived with grander ideas but poorer carpentry skills, so the British settlers' constructions were relatively rudimentary. And their farming skills were no better than those that already existed either.

And yet, a steady migration to Ireland began during these years which gathered pace in a way that hadn't been anticipated. And they didn't come just from England; there was a significant influx from Scotland. They came from all classes, with most leaving behind a harsh existence on a generally treeless lowland landscape, and arrived in Ireland with its woods, bountiful rivers and fertile land. So many took the relatively short trip from Scotland, in fact, that boats were almost continually crossing back and forth between the two coasts.

There is probably some exaggeration of the numbers that actually came to Ulster during the Plantations, because they are the result of guesswork in the first place. After all, only adult males were counted when any tally was taken. By 1620, however, there were an estimated 50,000 settlers across Ireland. By 1641, there may have been about 100,000 settlers in all from Britain, and most of these were in Leinster and Munster. But as many as 30,000 Scots may have migrated to Ulster in the decades leading up to 1641 and, while Ulster was an English-dominated plantation, the Scots set about carving an enclave that would have a massive influence on the future of the island.

A clear picture of what they left behind is given in James G. Leyburn's *The Scotch-Irish: A Social History*, which goes into colourful detail about the monotony of their diet, the team efforts needed simply to scrape a plough across the surface of a small field and the general filth which left the average life expectancy hovering at about 35 years of age.

Leyburn gives a vivid sense of the most bizarre superstitions. 'It was considered unlucky to wash the churns, a frog was put into the tubs to make the milk churn; the consistency of butter was thought to depend upon the number of hairs it contained.'

Life held many challenges.

Poor and barren soil ill-suited to agriculture; primitive methods; lack of education and of contact with people from other countries whose agricultural procedures were superior; superstition; constant raw weather which at any time might result in crop failure and famine; recurrence of plagues; and a steady round of wars, internal dissensions, theft of cattle, violence and lawlessness—these were the components of life in the humble annals of the poor farmer.

Frankly, anywhere else would sound like an attractive alternative. Ulster just happened to be closest. This meant that it was relatively easy for a man to bring his wife and children with him. Emigration to the European continent was the preserve of unmarried men, and as north America was settled it also attracted a disproportionate number of men. Ulster was close enough to bring a family, and it was close enough to return home too.

It was the Scottish who finally made the Plantations work, after decades of attempts by the English. Still, they would later be described in withering terms, such as these words of a minister: 'From Scotland came many, and from England not a few, yet from all of them generally the scum of both nations.'

Among the greater ironies, though, was that a great many of the Scots who arrived in Ireland were Gaelic speakers. While the Plantations were intended to attract lowland Scots, it did not prevent the Gaelic-speaking Highlanders from making their way over too.

The languages were still extremely similar in both the writing and the speaking. A lot of the Scottish soldiers would have been Gaelic speakers, and so settled with relative ease after the wars. Such was the lack of English spoken by many of the settlers that Gaelic-speaking ministers had to be imported to parishes. The only Gaelic Bible available to the Scots during the seventeenth and eighteenth centuries was printed in Irish.

For the planters, there was the ongoing danger posed by wood-kerns, dispossessed Irish, usually former soldiers, who formed armed bands of plunderers and who helped disabuse newcomers of the notion that all the natives had been killed off by war and famine. They were a regular menace, and when caught were often executed publicly after summary trials, although the Lord Deputy of Ireland, Francis Chichester, found what he considered to be a more practical use for the Irish, sending thousands of these 'idle swordsmen' off to serve in the Swedish army, which was then fighting in Poland. This also happened to be quite a useful method of getting them out of the way in case the Spanish returned to Irish shores to support them.

Yet, despite all this, the island actually entered into a period of relative peace. For 20 years Ireland was calm, which in turn fostered a stronger economy to add to a growing population, which by 1641 is estimated to have been about 2.1 million, up 700,000 since 1600. Not all the newcomers, it must be said, were English or Scots (Dutch and French also came to Ireland during this time) and not all were Protestant, with a number of Catholics moving to Ireland to escape the cruelties of religious persecution.

Such was the improvement in the Irish economy during the period leading up to 1641 (except for a brief downturn in 1628), that ports on the other side of the Irish Sea, such as Chester and Liverpool, grew on the back of it. Hides were then Ireland's chief export in an economy reliant on cows. In 1640, when things were said to be in something of a depression, an estimated 45,000 cattle were exported from Ireland. Most went to England, but some went as far as the new colonies in Virginia. The scale of the Irish enterprise was such that the English and Welsh lobbied for some protection against it.

Dublin was the one place on the island where people could visit to purchase imported and specialist goods. It meant that there was a steady flow of visitors, mostly English living in other parts of the country who came to pick up items such as tennis rackets, hats, gloves, looking glasses, spurs, stirrups and playing cards.

Along with the vital broadcloth that was the base material for most clothes, gold lace, velvet, satin and dyes were arriving from England for the wealthier settlers. Hops were imported for brewing, as was tobacco. Because they weren't exactly something that could be picked up off any passing salesman, there was also a flourishing trade in imported urinals.

There were other developments in the city. For instance, the first book produced in Dublin and Ireland had been the *Book of Common Prayer*, printed in 1551, and a printing trade developed during the 1600s, even if a relatively modest 109 titles in all were published between 1601 and 1641.

Theatre was also introduced to Ireland in a formal way, although, before that, it appears that London audiences could enjoy the thrill and thrust of the Irish wars, as recreated for them on the stage. From the early 1600s, the only surviving play about the subject is *The Famous Historye of the Life and Death of Captaine Thomas Stukeley, with His Marriage to Alderman Curteis Daughter, and Valiant Ending of His Life at the Battle of Alcazar.*

We don't know who wrote the play. The title gives a pretty good idea that whoever it was clearly wasn't precious about keeping his endings a secret.

Captain Thomas Stukeley was a real figure—a landowner in Ireland as well as a mercenary, rebel and all-round daredevil who at one point persuaded Queen Elizabeth 1 to give him ships so he could colonise Florida, only to take those vessels and go raiding French and Spanish boats off the Munster coast. He was clearly ripe for a dramatic take, but the play has been handed down in such an incoherent state that it's possible that we've actually been given a patchwork of plays. However, if it was played in any way as we see it now—and we cannot even be certain it was performed at all—then the audience would have enjoyed the spectacle of a Scots warrior arriving onstage with the head of Ulster chieftain Shane O'Neill as a peace offering to the English. Its politics were not exactly subtle.

The play would not have been staged in Dublin. Despite its long history of performance, Ireland had no dedicated theatres. Instead, the Gaelic noblemen might employ a retinue of performers, from the *filidh* (poets) to the *braigetóirí*—professional farters whose talents were in great demand.

Ireland's first recorded theatre production had been put on in the Great Hall of Dublin Castle on 7 September 1601, when the Nine Years War was still in full swing. Here, lit by candles, the Irish Lord Deputy, Charles Blount, better known as Lord Mountjoy, was among those who watched *Gorboduc*, a tale, in blank verse, of fratricide, civil war and rebellion and in which a character warns that 'with fire and sword thy native folk shall perish ... when noble men do fail in loyal troth, and subjects will be kings'. In the audience would have been a few of the native Irish. Two days later, Mountjoy rode out to engage the enemy. 'Mountjoy was doing more than entertaining his guests,' explains Christopher Marsh in *A History of Irish Theatre*, 'he was using the theatre to define the terms of war.'

Until a dedicated theatre was constructed, plays were put on privately in the great houses around the country. The first purpose-built theatre was completed by 1637 at Werburgh Street in Dublin on the instruction of the then new Lord Lieutenant, the Earl of Strafford, Thomas Wentworth. Plans were made to bring a company of actors and musicians from England, and lucky for them London was hit by an outbreak of plague, which forced the theatres there to close and its actors and playwrights to look elsewhere for work.

Historians are unsure of when the Werburgh Street Playhouse was first opened, or where exactly it was on the street. They do know that it was an indoor theatre that held perhaps 300 people but had, according to one eighteenth-century historian, 'a gallery and a pit, but no boxes' except for one for the Lord Lieutenant.

A member of Wentworth's circle, John Ogilby, was given the task of engaging a troupe, and went about it well. His story up to that point had already been somewhat colourful. When his father was imprisoned for failing to pay his debts, the young Ogilby had invested in a lottery, won it and used the winnings to bail out his father. However, his dream of being a dancer led to less fortune, when, as an apprentice, an ambitious leap went very wrong and he was left with a permanent limp.

Nevertheless, his enthusiasm for the theatre did not dim and as plague gripped London he encouraged some actors of great renown to move to Dublin. Most importantly, he secured the services of a writer, James Shirley. Shirley had been a Protestant minister until his conversion to Roman Catholicism quickly put paid to that career path. Becoming a playwright, he turned out to be quite prolific if not particularly important in the wider scheme of things. He had arrived at the tail end of a glorious period for English theatre, and is remembered more for aping the greatness of the Elizabethan playwrights—William Shakespeare and Christopher Marlowe among them—than for any special greatness of his own.

Shirley wrote four plays during his few years in Ireland, but by 1640, the original company had more or less disbanded and returned to London. However, on St Patrick's Day of that year, the first Irish-penned play was staged. Henry Burnell's *Landgartha* was an allegory of the gathering political problems in Ireland that were soon to have catastrophic consequences. Which is something not immediately made clear by its prologue, which is delivered by an Amazonian warrior with a battle-axe in her hand.

From this point on, it is largely a tale of misfortune for the building and those who worked in it. Its patron, Wentworth, fell foul of the law and was beheaded on trumped up charges of treason. The theatre itself then closed in 1641, after which the stage was used as a glorified cowshed until the building eventually fell into ruin.

And that same year, when rebellion broke out across Ireland, John Ogilby lost a fortune and almost lost his life when he was nearly blown up at Rathfarnham Castle, and again when he was shipwrecked while sailing back to England. Fortune continued to be cruel to him and he later lost a valuable library, a shop and a house in the Great Fire of London. Eventually, he recovered from all these setbacks to go on to become one of the most important mapmakers of his era.

James Shirley was not so fortunate. In 1666, the playwright and his second wife were driven from their home by the Great Fire of London and were both dead by the end of that day. They were said to have been killed by fright.

By that time, however, the Ireland they had left behind had suffered yet another of the major catastrophes that so regularly visited the place and its people. The rebellion of 1641 erupted in Ulster as a response to the taking of land from both the native Irish chiefs and some of the Old English, as well as because of the religious divide. The result was the so-called Confederate Catholics, an alliance between Irish rebels, Old English and Royalists fighting for the restoration of the English Crown, which by then had been overthrown. While it was a sometimes fractious alliance, with each part of it having different aims, it was successful enough that within less than a year it had control of all of Ireland with the exception of Dublin. That situation lasted almost the rest of the decade, despite various political and military attempts to fight back. But it was in 1649 that its defining moment came with the arrival of Oliver Cromwell.

The war had once again proved the island's boundless potential for great brutality, with massacres of settlers and terrible reprisals against the natives. In one massacre at Portadown Bridge in November of 1641, as many as 100 Protestant settlers were forced into the waters of the River Bann and drowned. Fleeing columns of refugees were then set upon on the road, where they were reportedly robbed, stripped and then released naked into the winter conditions.

In all, it's estimated that perhaps 5,000 settlers died in the opening months of the rebellion. (Although it is thought that as many Catholics died in reprisal attacks.) It seems hard to exaggerate such events, but the English propagandists managed it when reporting the settlers' predicament, sending word back that 100,000 settlers had been killed.

Cromwell came to Ireland in 1649 and began a campaign that was savage but effective. War and famine took hold of the island to a ferocious extent. The scale of the catastrophe that followed—and the manner in which it was inflicted—was extraordinary. There was a depopulation of land, the destruction of livestock and land, and terrible hunger, so that food stocks needed to be imported as land prices crashed. As if that wasn't enough, there were outbreaks of the plague in each of the years between 1650 and 1654, when it would emerge in the early summer and dissipate by September only to re-emerge again the following May. When all these conditions—hunger, war, disease—came together they had an appalling effect. For example, Limerick was besieged by Cromwell's forces during 1650–51 and by the time the city surrendered, about 5,000 were already dead. The victims were not solely among the city's inhabitants and defenders, 2,000 of the Cromwellian forces died during the siege, mostly from disease.

Between 1641 and 1672, through death or exile, the population of Ireland dropped by an estimated 400,000, or almost one-fifth. As the historian Robin Clifton has written of the wars in England, Scotland and Ireland, 'among the three kingdoms it was only in Ireland, it seems, that civil war unleashed humanity's capacity for wholesale and pitiless slaughter'.

It was Cromwell's campaign that finally established British control of Ireland. At the beginning of the 1600s, Catholics had owned 90 per cent of the land. By the time the war began, Protestants had increased their collective stake to 40 per cent. Within a few decades, Protestants owned 90 per cent.

That happened because of an ambitious and relatively successful confiscation of Catholic lands and the resettlement of the Catholic landowners to the western edge of the country. Some

Parliamentarians (the Civil War victors) had suggested that the *entire* Irish population be deported west of the Shannon, and while this wasn't actually carried out in such a wholesale way, a great many of them were hemmed into the western part of the island. Connacht was chosen because it was far from Scotland and the Continent, and had what was considered to be a natural defensive line in the River Shannon.

Lands were confiscated from Catholics to be given to Protestant landowners and retired soldiers. In Connacht, they were taken from the native chieftains so that they could be divided among the other Catholics who were being uprooted and transplanted.

The Irish were to be penned into Connacht and Munster's Co. Clare, because the land wasn't particularly valuable there anyway. And where it was—such as in coastal areas—then it was to be kept for the Protestants. It was also suggested that all the Presbyterians of Counties Down and Antrim be moved to Kilkenny, Tipperary and Waterford, but this was decided against and instead the Catholics were to take the brunt of the pain.

A land survey was carried out, led by William Petty, a scientist, surveyor and religious zealot, who only took on the job having pointed out the errors of the man previously charged with carrying it out. Petty dispatched some of the many idle soldiers to the countryside, giving them instructions on how to measure the land and telling them to use chains to take distances.

Twenty-two counties were surveyed, with impressive swiftness and accuracy. Petty's reward was to have to chase up his employers for the money owed to him until he was eventually given several thousand acres of land in lieu of the cash. Still, it was ultimately a profitable job for him. He ended up with cash, a title and a large chunk of Co. Kerry. By the time he was done with his work, Ireland was probably the most accurately surveyed country in all of Europe. That statistic, though, was of absolutely no consolation to the Catholic landowners who were then summarily robbed of that land and transplanted west of the Shannon.

The settlements destroyed the Irish landowning classes, but they were not the sole victims. As large numbers of people moved in from England and Scotland, Catholics were removed from towns, sometimes in entire professions, such as when all the Catholic shoemakers of Dublin were expelled in 1657. That approach hurt the economies of Galway, Waterford, Limerick and Cork, because to force out the Catholic merchants could hardly be done smoothly and without any effect on trading. If other cities were stymied by the impact of the Cromwellian settlements, Dublin—having resisted rebellion and solidified its economic links with England—did very well out of it, flourishing from the 1660s onwards to the point where it became the second-largest city in Britain and Ireland.

Others either left or were transported away, such as the 12,000 Irish—most of them poor—who were shipped off to the West Indies to work on the plantations there. Almost three times as many were permitted to leave and serve in foreign armies. About 15,000 went to Spain, but others went to Austria, France and Venice.

And the cruelties of the Cromwellian settlements sometimes had a certain historical irony. Among those who lost their land was Edmund Spenser's grandson, who had been born Catholic but had renounced it. In fact, he'd only been seven years old at the time that the rebellion broke out, so could hardly be charged with complicity.

Who replaced the Catholics? The bulk were former soldiers and 'adventurers', who had been promised land in return for getting involved in the Cromwellian campaign in the first place. Following the war, 12,000 of Cromwell's army were given land in lieu of wages, with 7,500 opting to settle and the rest selling their land. This was far fewer than the 36,000 estates originally planned. The initial idea had also been for the soldiers to be settled in strategic positions, most obviously along the borders of Connacht, but not enough of them settled to make this effective. And just for good measure, for all their supposed disdain of the

Irish, a lot of them married Catholic Irishwomen even though it was officially prohibited.

Among those soldiers were many Scots, who added to the stocks who had already settled in Ulster during the Plantations. But there was another major migration of Scots in the 1680s and 1690, when they fled a lowland famine, for the first time making the Scottish, or their descendants, a majority in the province. Many of these new immigrants were zealously Presbyterian.

Curiously, after the immediate impact of the settlements, which had left the Catholic population with only 9 per cent of the land, with the death of Oliver Cromwell and the restoration of the English Crown in 1660 under Charles II, Catholics began to get their land back so that they eventually came to own almost a quarter of it.

Nevertheless, by the close of the 1600s, a transformation of Ireland had well and truly occurred. Across the island, there had been a drastic alteration in land ownership that would take centuries to be undone, and even then only partially. There are many people living in new housing estates across Ireland whose contract stipulates that they pay a nominal fee to a landowner whose ancestors would have received the land back in the seventeenth century.

And in the north-east of Ireland there had been such a radical change in the population that a great many people who live there still describe themselves as Ulster-Scots. Some claim to speak a dialect they also call Ulster-Scots. Many cling fast to an identity that could be considered neither English, nor Irish and not exactly Scottish. When James I had planned his uniquely 'British' population in Ireland, he would never have understood just how that would come to pass.

Chapter 6 ⌒

ITALIAN CHIPPERS AND LITTLE JERUSALEM: OTHER IMMIGRATIONS

I rish visitors to Italy will no doubt have noticed that its national dish is not burger and chips. You do not swing onto Rome's Via del Corso to be met by the smell of boiling oil. You do not sit down for dinner, and choose an antipasto of batter burger and onion rings.

Which has always made it somewhat curious that the Italians in Ireland became renowned for their chippers, and that many of the names that were serving fish and chips half a century ago will still be serving snack boxes to peckish or drunken Irish this and every weekend.

It began sometime in the 1880s, when an Italian, Giuseppe Cervi, stepped off an American-bound boat that had stopped in Cobh and kept walking until he reached Dublin. There, he worked as a labourer until he earned enough money to buy a coal-fired cooker and a hand-cart, from which he sold chips outside pubs.

Soon after, he found a permanent spot on Great Brunswick Street (now Pearse Street), where his wife Palma would ask customers *'Uno di questo, uno di quello?'*, meaning 'one of this and one of the other?' In doing so, Palma helped to coin a Dublin phrase, 'one and one', which is still a common way of asking for fish and chips. The shop, meanwhile, had launched an industry.

Much of what is known about the history of the chipper is detailed in the wonderful work of John K. Walton, a professor of

Social History at the University of Central Lancashire. In 1994, he wrote a book, *Fish and Chips and the British Working Class, 1870–1940*, and it is an invaluable addition to the admittedly small library of chipper histories.

In it, we learn that, by 1909, there were 20 fish and chip shops in Dublin, serving a population of only 290,000. This, though, was nothing compared with the size of the trade in British cities, where the relationship between chippers and Italians originated. In 1905, there was a fish and chip shop for every 400 citizens of Leeds and Bradford.

The chipper had first become popular in the north of England, as a happy amalgam of fried fish and cooked potato trades that had grown separately during the mid-1800s. 'It is not clear which area, and still less which individual, deserves the credit for bringing about the momentous marriage of fish and chips,' writes Walton. 'This is a matter of murky and probably insoluble dispute.' However, it is guessed that it happened sometime between the 1860s and 1890s.

It was in Scotland that the Italians began to make the fish and chip trade their own. Why they were so taken by the business isn't clear, though Walton suggests that it may have been because they saw the fish and chip shops of London as they passed through there on their way north. With Italians leading the way, Scotland was home to 4,500 chippers by 1914. In Glasgow alone, an estimated 800,000 fish suppers were being sold every week. Naturally, the shops often doubled as ice-cream parlours.

With the Italian immigrants to Ireland, then, came the chip shops. These were not the first Italians to make an impression in Ireland. Stucco workers had been imported to work on the big houses of the country; the tiling, glasswork and ornamental woodwork in Belfast's glorious Crown Bar were created by Italians moonlighting in between working on Catholic churches. Others were brought here as musicians and dancers.

But for individual impact few Italian immigrants could rival

Charles Bianconi. Originally a purveyor of gilded frames, Bianconi realised that there had to be an alternative to lugging the goods around on his back. So, in 1815, he set up a coach service, with the first route running from Clonmel, Co. Tipperary to Cahir, Co. Waterford. By the middle of the century, his routes criss-crossed the island and he had become a very wealthy man indeed. By the time Bianconi died, in 1875, the railway was well on its way to killing the coach business, but he had been responsible for the country's first integrated transport system.

Still, it is through their chippers that the Italian population in Ireland served up an example of how a relatively small number of newcomers could imprint themselves on the national culture, psyche and, in this case, stomach.

The Italian chipper families in Ireland almost all come from a district of six villages in the province of Frosinone, and they originally came here as the subdivision of land at home led to mass migration from rural Italy. Families such as the Borzas, Caffellos and Macaris are still the names on the Guinness-blackened tongues of Saturday nights.

These Italians came to Dublin via Paris, then Scotland or resorts in the south of England, where they would no doubt have seen the success their compatriots had had in the fish and chip trade there. In Ireland, they managed to replicate that success, although some regions proved hard to crack. Walton points out that, given how the migration chain would have gone from Scotland through the north of Ireland, it is odd that Belfast 'provided inhospitable soil for Italian fish friers in the early twentieth century'. Belfast remained resolutely keen on oysters and shrimps instead of fried fish. The post-pub trade in oysters has clearly not lasted.

Instead, it was Dublin and Cork in which the chippers first took hold, although it's worth noting that Ireland's well-known fish and chip shop, Beshoff, was set up by a Ukrainian immigrant, Ivan Beshov, who had taken part in the 1905 mutiny on the

Potemkin and fled west through Turkey and London, until he landed in Ireland where he was first arrested and interned in the Curragh camp on suspicion of being a German spy. Once he became free, he set up a chip shop with the help of Italian friends, and had to restart after it was destroyed in a bombing of Dublin's North Strand by the Germans in 1941. It went on to become something of a Dublin institution. When he died in 1987, his birth certificate said he was 102 years old, but he had insisted that he was 104.

The Chinese in Ireland, also a small population for most of the twentieth century, had an impact on the taste buds and street fronts of a great many Irish towns and villages. The Chinese migrants of the 1950s to 1970s came mostly from Hong Kong, leaving their homes because of economic pressures brought about by a collapse in the local rice farming industry. They travelled through Britain and on to the north of Ireland, because their status as Commonwealth citizens allowed them free movement until a change in the law in 1962 limited the flow of immigrants.

With them came the Chinese restaurant that had grown in popularity in Britain during the post-war years. Ireland's first opened in 1957, in a house on Leeson Street. There are now about 6,000 Chinese restaurants in the country.

The first Chinese restaurant opened only a year after the first Indian restaurant, the Golden Orient, was also opened on Leeson Street. Its proprietor, Mike Butt, was an East African Indian who had come to Ireland from Kenya, and upon opening he found that most Irish people just wanted to order steak. So he served steak, but the Golden Orient survived as an Indian restaurant for those looking for a little culinary adventure. The number of Indian restaurants did not explode in the way that Chinese restaurants did, and certainly not as they did in the UK, although this is largely down to how little Asian migration there was to Ireland. Still, the two countries share certain trends. Even now, when most people in Britain or Ireland go for Indian food, they are probably eating in a

Bangladeshi restaurant, as it is they who have popularised the cuisine of the subcontinent of which their country used to be part. Although, this is not always true. Some are run by Pakistanis.

All of these culinary offcuts might seem like a bit of a diversion, but they also serve as peculiar reminders of how a small influx of migrants—even a single migrant—can have an impact on a national culture that couldn't possibly have been foreseen at the time.

———

Throughout the centuries, there have been small numbers of people coming to Ireland from other countries. Some came en masse—and often left en masse shortly afterwards—and others dribbled in over time.

Until the last couple of decades of the twentieth century, they were most likely to arrive as refugees, fleeing a war, a failed uprising or religious persecution. In fact, the original refugees (or, at least, those who gave the world the word) were the Huguenots, French Protestants whose influence here may have been relatively minor but it was still enough for them to leave behind family lines, a few surnames, a couple of street names and an industry—linen— which the north-east of Ireland was to do very well out of.

How the Huguenots got their name is not known for sure. It may have been a name flung at them in the sixteenth century by their enemies, who associated them with Swiss Calvinists led by a fellow called Besançon Hugues. Or it may have come from a Flemish/German word *Huisgenooten*, or 'house fellows', or a Swiss/German word *Eidgenossen* ('oath fellows') that had to do with how they studied secretly in each other's homes. Whatever the case, by 1550 it was being used by French Catholics to describe religious heretics. And, as occasionally happens, the insult was later co-opted by the targets as their own.

Anyway, that name was banned by the Edict of Nantes in 1598, in order to protect the French Protestants who at this time were supported by a king who had been born Protestant but converted to Catholicism for purely political reasons. And they needed protecting, because in the previous decades they'd been at the rough end of some gruesome acts, the most infamous being the St Bartholomew's Day massacre of 1572, during which several thousand Huguenots were killed when they flocked to Paris to celebrate the wedding of one of their leading figures to the French king's Catholic sister.

As dawn broke on 24 August, Catholic soldiers armed with clubs, pikes, swords and firearms stormed the houses of Protestants and, not wanting to strain themselves by dragging them downstairs, often just threw their occupants out the windows. It was the beginning of a day-long slaughter of men, women and children. They drowned them, stabbed them and hanged them. The Seine ran red with blood.

Over the course of the century, the Huguenots' religious freedoms were gradually eroded by Catholic kings until they began to seek refuge in great numbers. At first, Ireland wasn't their destination. There were two waves of migrations to England, but only a smattering of Huguenots in Ireland until the 1660s, when the Lord Lieutenant at the time, James Butler, Duke of Ormond, decided that the Huguenot's supposed 'energy, integrity, competence, skills and business acumen' would be just the thing to 'inspire the general Irish population to habits of hard work, sobriety and thrift'. Plus they would likely prove loyal to an English Crown only recently restored after the Cromwell years.

So, he drew up the Act for Encouraging Protestant Strangers and Others to Establish Themselves in Ireland. It was partially successful, with a brief inflow of Huguenots between 1662 and 1670. However, it took some particularly brutal violence against the Huguenots to kickstart a larger migration to Ireland.

The number of French in Dublin suddenly became noticeable,

even if there was only 650 Huguenots in the capital by 1686. Still, they proved useful, most notably in battle where Huguenots joined the side of William of Orange in defeating the forces of the Catholic James II at the Battles of the Boyne and Aughrim in 1690 and 1691. In fact, the second-in-command (second to William of Orange, of course) of the Williamite forces at the Battle of the Boyne was a Huguenot, the 74-year-old Frederick Schomberg, the Duke of Schomberg. As it happens, he wasn't a migrant to Ireland—as a refugee he had gone to Germany—but landed purely for military reasons. However, he joined the great bulk of William of Orange's army in not being English, because Danes, Dutch, French, Swedes and Prussians all fought in that battle. And Schomberg died in it, struck down while riding through the river.

The Huguenots had a grander moment of glory in Ireland. A vital defeat of the Catholics came at Aughrim, where 40,000 troops in all fought, 7,000 of whom were dead by the end of that day. It is the largest battle ever to have taken place in Ireland and the eventual victory has long been credited to a charge by Huguenot cavalry, led by one Henri Massue de Ruvigny.

Battles, though, were not the general experience of the Huguenots in Ireland. Between 1692 and 1722, their migration from France happened in earnest: 200,000 left their homes, with 50,000 of them ending up in England. About 10,000 arrived in Ireland, and the plan was to settle them in organised schemes. After his successes at the Battle of Aughrim and a subsequent siege of Limerick, de Ruvigny drew up plans for settlements in towns around the country, including Kilkenny, Youghal, Belfast, Lisburn, Dublin and the one that would eventually prove most successful, Portarlington.

That Co. Laois town, in fact, is pretty much a French creation. There was a scattering of people there, and there had been some work done by the English during the mid-1600s, when the town was named in honour of a Lord Arlington. But it was never actually a port at all—there was a small quay at the River Barrow and there was also a fort with which it may have become confused.

The first Huguenot settlers at Portarlington were disbanded officers, several of whom had been wounded in the Irish wars. They were followed by others from professional and agricultural backgrounds. They struggled to settle. Colonists arrived too quickly for construction to keep pace. As well as houses, they lacked a church (quite a priority, you would think, for religious refugees) and key professionals such as a doctor and a schoolteacher. Many of those had already been nearly bankrupted by the combination of the journey and the expense of trying to establish an Irish home. They begged for donations of seeds to get themselves going. When they died, there was no dedicated burial ground.

Portarlington survived, and eventually thrived, but elsewhere, the Huguenot impact faded rather quickly. As the historian Raymond Hylton put it in *Ireland's Huguenots and their Refuge*, his comprehensive telling of the Huguenot story in Ireland, 'Before the turn of the nineteenth century every single Huguenot community in Ireland was well on the road to absorption; and in many instances had already arrived there and become the stuff of regional folklore.'

But they left an imprint on the island nonetheless. It is in some of the street names, such as Dublin's D'Olier Street, after Jeremiah D'Olier, a third-generation Huguenot from a family of goldsmiths, who was High Sheriff of Dublin in 1788. And there is a physical (and metaphysical) reminder right in the heart of Dublin, on a corner of St Stephen's Green, where a small Huguenot graveyard is gated, protected and hemmed in by the city. There is a graveyard in Cork City too, which has survived a couple of planning applications that would have built over it.

They also left a mark on the economy. The Huguenots proved very useful in the wine trade, and they are also credited with helping to popularise gardening. However, it is to the North's linen trade that they made their greatest contribution. Once he had seen off the Catholic forces, William of Orange rewarded the North by removing taxes on its linen, mainly because it didn't pose a threat to any English industry, unlike the trade in cattle, wool and dairy products which were treated less favourably. A fellow called Louis Crommelin, who had escaped to Holland, was invited to bring a group of Huguenot weavers to Ireland. He accepted the offer, and in 1698 brought many people and a thousand looms. The industry flourished for over two centuries until eventually going into irreversible decline in the 1960s.

The Huguenots were not the only Protestant refugees to come to Ireland during this period of religious upheaval in Europe. In 1709, as the Huguenot migration to Ireland was in full swing, there was also a brief and mostly temporary influx of Protestant refugees from the German Palatine region. Here again, the French have been blamed for their movement, although this time through attacking the Protestants in Germany. However, the Palatines might just as easily be considered economic migrants as their migration coincided with a vicious winter that proved one too many for an agricultural people, many of whom were vine-growers.

The British queen, Anne, came to their aid. She sent a fleet to Rotterdam to bring refugees to England; 13,500 in all were transported. It quickly transpired that 3,000 of these were actually Catholics, and they were immediately dispatched home again.

Those who were the genuine article weren't entirely welcome in London either, with one pamphlet asking why the Crown should raise £300,000

. . . for a crowd of blackguards who could have lived happily in their own land had not the laziness of their disposition and the report of our own generosity drawn them out of it. As to the pretence to come hither purely for the exercise of their religion, there was nothing in it, though some were induced to relieve them on account of their pretended persecution.

Those who made it to London would mostly have been hoping for transportation to the colonies of the New World. Some did indeed go to North Carolina and New York, but 3,000 of them— 821 families—probably got something of a surprise when they were sent to Ireland.

The government offered Irish landlords a very substantial £25,000 subsidy to anyone who would allow Palatines to settle on their land, and several took up the offer. The Palatines received 8 acres per man, woman and child, at a rent of 5 s per acre (compared with the 35 s per acre paid by the Irish). Each family was also to be given money for seven years to buy utensils and tools.

It was a failed experiment. Within three years, two-thirds of the original settlers had abandoned Ireland, returning either to England or all the way back to Germany, some apparently having grown disgruntled with their landlords. By August 1712, 254 of the original families remained in Ireland and there was a great deal of unhappiness expressed about the whole affair. For instance, there were complaints in the Irish Parliament about 'the load of debt which the bringing over of useless and indigent Palatines had brought'.

Not every attempt was doomed, however, with a settlement in Co. Limerick surviving thanks predominantly to the efforts of the landowner Sir Thomas Southwell of Castle Matrix near Rathkeale, who put much of his own money into trying to help about 130 families to establish themselves on his land. And where they held on, their culture persisted longer than the Huguenots' managed. German remained their language for a couple of generations at least, and there are various references to the continued distinctiveness of the Palatine culture towards the end of the 1700s. And while relatively few Palatines ultimately stayed in Ireland, there were enough to leave a few surnames.

Among them Switzer, Bowen, a handful of Teskeys in Limerick and a few Millers who can trace their ancestry to Muller.

For a couple of centuries afterwards, Ireland proved to be far less of an attraction to refugees—if it had ever really been much of an attraction in the first place. There was an inpouring of Jews towards the end of the 1800s—but we'll come back to this later in the chapter. And the world wars had a minor impact, with small numbers coming to the island during both of them.

During the First World War, though, perhaps a thousand Belgians landed in Ireland, a minority from the many families that had left for Great Britain and Ireland (then, of course, still part of that empire). Some went into civilian homes, others were housed in workhouses. That there were few compared with the numbers that went to Britain was apparently because many of them refused to travel across to Ireland as they had heard that the sea was mined. (It was.)

The Belgian incomers were considered to be in three classes, according to newspaper reports at the time which named these as 'workmen in trades in which labour is wanted, workmen in other trades [in which, presumably, labour was not wanted] and professional and business men, shopkeepers, and others of a similar kind'. A committee set up to examine their needs suggested that work should be found for these people, but that there had to be a level of common sense. It would be bad policy, as a report put it, 'to set up Belgian dressmakers in competition with our already long-suffering seamstresses'.

As the war came to an end and Belgium was eventually liberated, notices appeared in the Irish press asking Belgians not to suddenly up sticks and return home, but to wait until official repatriation. In February 1919, 500 Belgians left Dublin on a boat home. Their trip had been paid for, and they'd been given a free luggage allowance up to 300 lb per person as well as a gift from the people behind the Belgian Gift Shop, which had raised funds on their behalf.

During the First World War there had also been some concern that English and Scottish fugitives from conscription were running away to Ireland (where there was no conscription) and that there was little being done to tackle the problem. Many were believed to have gone to Belfast, where a Scot was considered to be far less noticeable and would have had a better chance of getting work. There were still an estimated 500 men hiding from conscription in Dublin in 1917, but this was far fewer than the 5,000 one MP claimed were in the city.

During the Second World War a small number of people moved to Ireland. Curiously, our wartime isolation has long been blamed for developing an insularity and cultural stasis during what was referred to as the Emergency. It has more recently been argued that, by attracting artistic refugees from Germany and France, it in fact led to a brief flourishing of the arts in Ireland—or in Dublin at least. It suddenly became an attractive place for such refugees as well as for conscientious objectors.

But the number of people who came to Ireland was relatively small, and this was primarily down to the newly independent State's reluctance to take in even Jewish refugees in the years after the war, when the scale of the Holocaust was clear. It was only when the Irish government signed up to the Geneva Convention in 1956 that it began to accept its duties in this regard, and that same year 530 Hungarians arrived as escapees from their uprising against the Soviets.

The events in Hungary had already been watched keenly in Ireland, as they were throughout the West, and had led to some excitement. Dublin dockers refused to handle Russian goods; church-gate collections had raised money for Hungarian aid; four tonnes of cheese was donated by a creamery; and schoolboys marched in Limerick, flinging an effigy of Russian premier Marshal Bulganin off a bridge and into the Shannon.

Ireland agreed to take some of the refugees, and at short notice threw up a camp at the Knockalisheen barracks, Co. Clare. It was such short notice, in fact, that the place was draughty, leaky and had little furniture. Nevertheless, on Sunday, 25 November 1956, less than a month after the uprising had begun, 35 families arrived at the camp, the youngest member only one week old. The *Irish Times* reported how, on arrival at Shannon, the child's parents were first off the plane, but as they ran across the tarmac the baby's bottle dropped and broke.

Among the arrivals were a shoemaker, a lawyer, a boxer and three chauffeurs. There was also one case of TB, which explains why they were immediately quarantined for two weeks before being allowed to wander into the town beside their camp.

By the end of December the numbers at the camp, under the care of the Irish Red Cross, had risen to 526. They stayed in what were still reported to be leaking huts, and during the winter several children developed bronchitis thanks to the conditions. However, certain necessities of life continued as is clear by how, on one Saturday in December, there were three weddings in the camp.

The Hungarians did more than simply make do. They showed ingenuity, sending home lemons and limes which relatives could sell on the black market, and tapping into the electricity service to try to get light after the midnight switch-off. They also built up a small local market for their handicrafts.

In April 1957, 271 of the adults went on hunger strike in protest at their being refused a chance to move on to Canada, the US, Argentina and Australia as some said they had been promised. On 13 June, they wrote to the US Congress complaining of the conditions. So, their Irish hosts agreed to move them to a new camp at Templemore, Co. Tipperary. Once it was kitted out, the Hungarians decided not to go. They had, they explained, made friends and, in some cases, found jobs in the area. Plus, they added, they'd borrowed a lot of things from the local people and would have to return them all if they were to move. They also had their handiwork industry to think about. Meanwhile, the local businesses were also opposed to their moving, given that the refugees had brought in about £1,500 in revenue.

The Irish Red Cross, an organisation with a long-standing reputation for generosity and kindness of spirit, began to lose patience. Its general secretary complained that 200 of the original refugees were actually communist sympathisers.

Gradually, the camp was disbanded. By August 1957, just 350 refugees remained. By October, that was down to 200. A number of the men then managed to get work in England while, in September 1958, 142 refugees went to Canada, with 61 who had been rejected by the Canadian authorities rehoused in Ireland.

In December 1958, the camp was officially closed, although a family of six and a 17-year-old remained its sole occupants. During their time in Ireland, 24 children had been born to the Hungarians and only one death had been reported.

During the 1990s, Knockalisheen once again came to be used as an accommodation for those seeking refugee status in Ireland, although the wooden huts had been replaced by more modern buildings. As for the Hungarians, some had remained in Ireland, putting down roots, having families and waiting another 30 years before the fall of communism in Hungary.

A couple of decades later, when speaking to the *Irish Times*, one eastern European gave a sense of the different perspectives between immigrants and the Irish at the time:

> Coming here from a Communist country was quite a shock. For a start, you must understand that the image that people have here of the East is simply lies, propaganda, the image of lines of people queuing for everything, of terrible poverty— when I came here first I had never seen streets like Gardiner Street [in Dublin]. I had never seen beggars.

Despite the not altogether satisfactory experience of the Hungarians, they were only the first of several small groups to travel to Ireland. In 1974, when the coup that brought Colonel Augusto Pinochet to power in that country led to an outflow of political opponents, Chilean refugees were taken into Ireland, with the government at first agreeing to 12 families, who would be considered permanent rather than temporary refugees.

In the end, about 120 people came to Ireland, and we would know a lot more about their daily lives here if the relevant files hadn't almost entirely been lost. However, one document does remain, which shows how the Minister for Justice at the time, Patrick Cooney, believed that even this small group shouldn't be allowed in at all. 'Our society is less cosmopolitan than that of western European countries generally and, in consequence, the absorption of even a limited number of foreigners of this kind could prove extremely difficult.' He was more concerned that among them would be 'left-wing activists' who might gravitate towards the Provisional IRA.

The Chileans were located in houses in several parts of the country, with about 40 settling in Galway, although their names were withheld from the press—understandable given Pinochet's habit of murdering his opponents' family members. They faced a few problems. Among them was a little geographical confusion on the part of their hosts. A Chilean couple in the west of Ireland later told the *Irish Times*: 'Sometimes people would say something like "Oh, Chile. Yes, I was in Africa once", while another man asked me what language I spoke, and I said Spanish. He said, "Oh yes, I knew Chile was in Spain."'

More seriously, as with the arrival of the Hungarians almost two decades before them, there hadn't been a great deal of forward planning put in before the Chileans landed. There was little consideration given to how their experiences in Chile might have left them needing specialist help. 'Many of us had been in prison, or had been expelled from our country,' one later explained, 'and in these cases we were often in bad physical condition—it is not generally recognised that political prisoners are almost always tortured. There was no medical care, no psychological care, the language especially was difficult.'

A government-backed scheme trained some to be welders, but English language classes were not provided at first, and were limited later on, so the newcomers struggled to find jobs. Plus, they considered themselves temporary refugees, waiting for the moment when political changes would allow them to return home. Indeed, by the late 1980s, many of the group had left Ireland, either because of the difficulties they had in settling or to take advantage of an amnesty offered by Pinochet's regime.

After the Chileans, other groups of refugees were accepted into Ireland: 212 Vietnamese boat people came here in 1979, all but 40 of them children. (Among the group was one family that had 13 kids.) Actually, the State only took them in after having refused to take in Vietnamese refugees twice before that, but ended up accepting them largely because Ireland was then holding the presidency of the EU and needed to be seen to do something positive.

The anthropologist Mark Maguire has written about this and points out that there wasn't a single Vietnamese dictionary in Ireland at the time—not much help given that the refugees were spread across the country, sometimes in very small groups, and that they would have been illiterate in their own language never mind having to try to learn English. During the 1980s they resettled in Dublin where they have established a small community that works mainly in the Chinese take-away business. Family reunification schemes helped bolster their numbers. In 1998, 200 Vietnamese were given visas to come to Ireland and reunite with some of those they had last seen before they left for Ireland in the late 1970s.

These 'programme refugees' were later followed by 26 Iranian Baha'i who arrived in the country in 1985 and over 600 Bosnians who came to Ireland during the Balkan conflict of the early 1990s. Individual circumstances never being straightforward, 42 Bosnians were given financial help in 1997 when they asked to return home again. And out of these, three were helped out again when they took up their right to return to Ireland.

And while they would in no way be counted as foreigners, there was also a steady stream of Northern Irish Catholics between 1969 and 1972; an estimated 3,000 in total moved south during these early years of the Troubles.

———

Yet, it is Ireland's decision to refuse certain refugees entry that put at odds the country's claim to be a Land of the Welcomes during its early years as an independent state. In the years leading to the Second World War it went to some lengths to avoid accepting Jewish refugees. Ireland was hardly alone in its refusal to accept Jews even among the Allied nations, but it continued to stonewall applications both during and after the war to such an extent that it would eventually be accused of being more hospitable to escaping war criminals than their victims.

This was despite the fact that there was a healthy Jewish community in Ireland by that stage, to the point where Dublin had its own 'Little Jerusalem'. Even if it was a *very* little Jerusalem.

The earliest reference to Jews in Ireland comes in a 1079 entry in the Annals of Inisfallen. 'Five Jews came from over sea with gifts to Tairdelbach, and they were sent back again over sea.' They may have been merchants and it's been suggested that this was an early example of anti-Semitism, a bad start for the Irish in their relationship with the Jews. We don't know, because the Annals don't follow up on their story.

There are occasional mentions of Jewish names in documents that followed the Anglo-Norman invasion in the twelfth century, and it's thought that there may have been a Jewish community in Ireland by the mid-1200s when King Henry III made a reference to the Jews in the country. A couple of hundred years later, there was a trickle of immigration from Jews known as the Sephardim, descendants of Jews who had been expelled from Spain en masse in 1492. But it wasn't until the mid-1600s that Dublin's first synagogue was built. For about a century after that, synagogues were usually located close to glassworks, so many Jews must have worked in that trade.

Ireland's Jewish population began to grow in the nineteenth century. Between 1820 and 1875, Litvak Jews from north and eastern Europe arrived as part of a wave of a population movement triggered by the Napoleonic Wars. Some ended up living in tenements in Chancery Lane, off Bride Street, described in one unpublished memoir as 'a little square wherein stood the police station, joining the other foreigners—Italian organ-grinders, bear leaders, one-man-band operators, and makers of small, cheap plaster casts of saints of the Catholic church'.

Proving that immigrants aren't always a monolithic group, the newcomers were not immediately welcomed by Dublin's small but established Jewish population that was then made up of 'English' Jews. The historian Cormac Ó Gráda's *Jewish Ireland in the Age of Joyce* tells us that this was based on the trusty class divide. The newcomers were seen as 'rather ignorant and uncouth' by a Jewish community that was concerned with integrating into the local community as best it could.

The overall Jewish population, though, was small enough for most of the 1800s. It was only in the last couple of decades of that century that it really began to lift. By 1891, there were almost 2,000 Jews in Ireland, concentrated mainly in Dublin. For instance, in 1891 there were still only 282 Jews in the six counties that now comprise Northern Ireland, 164 males and 118 females. Almost all were in Belfast. There was one, lone Jew in Tyrone.

However, the Jewish population in Ireland doubled again over the following decade. Of this, 2,000 were in Dublin (there was a grand total of 15 Jews in all of Connacht in 1901, all but one of whom was in Sligo). Over a couple of decades, the influx of Jews into Ireland was sudden and unprecedented. Traditionally it has been explained as having been triggered by the Russian pogroms that during that time led to 150,000 Jews arriving in Britain, and between 1880 and 1914 led to the migration of two million Russian Jews in all. Another historian, Dermot Keogh, writes of one man who took his family to Ireland, left his two children at his brother's music shop in Patrick Street in Cork, and returned home to Lithuania only to be killed in the pogroms. However, Ó Gráda has argued that the Lithuanian Jews who came to Ireland were mostly economic migrants.

Those that landed in Ireland came mostly from the Lithuanian province of Kovno Gubernia. In fact, the core of the Dublin and Cork communities came from what was described as a 'rather derelict little place called Akmijan'. In Dublin, their arrival led to the growth of the so-called Little Jerusalem to the south of the city, around Portobello, where there were Jewish businesses, a school and a slaughterhouse.

As far back as 1828, Daniel O'Connell had assured the Jewish liberation movement that 'Ireland has claims on your ancient race, as it is the only Christian Country that I know of unsullied by any act of persecution against the Jews.' If it was true in the first place, in 1904 it was corrected.

In that year, there were 25 Jewish families living in Limerick, most of them around a single street and most of them small-time businesspeople. Some Catholic shopkeepers approached the local director of the Redemptorist order, Father John Creagh, and expressed their concern at the competition posed by the Jewish shops. The resentment seems to have stemmed from an instalment payment system run by Jewish shopkeepers, although an investigation the previous year had cleared them of any wrong-doing. But it piqued Creagh's interest which may have been compounded by a belief that some troubles the Redemptorists were having in France were thanks to the Jews there.

Creagh was a 33-year-old who had been described by one newspaper as an 'athletic, clean-built "figure of a man", with the

characteristic cheerfulness and frankness of a son of the soil'.
In the pulpit, however, the cheerfulness was fully deluged by
the frankness. He was a powerful and popular preacher, who
attracted large and delighted crowds. He had made a name for
himself by railing against the evils of alcohol in the city. When he
turned his ferocity on the Jews, it was always going to have an
impact.

So, in January 1904 he spoke about Limerick's Jews, first
reminding the congregation of the Jews' responsibility for the
crucifixion of Jesus and then continuing:

> Nowadays, they dare not kidnap and slay Christian children,
> but they will not hesitate to expose them to a longer and even
> more cruel martyrdom by taking the clothes off their back and
> the bit out of their mouths.
>
> Twenty years ago and less Jews were known only by name and
> evil repute in Limerick. They were sucking the blood of other
> nations, but those nations rose up and turned them out and
> they came to our land to fasten themselves on us like leeches,
> and to draw our blood when they had been forced away from
> other countries. They have, indeed, fastened themselves upon
> us. And now the question is whether or not we allow them to
> fasten themselves still more upon us, until we and our children
> are the victims of their rapacity.

Creagh went on at some length to describe how the Jews had
'wormed themselves into every form of business', going into great
detail about their supposed rapacious business methods, how
they preyed on women and the blind. Creagh effectively called for
a boycott of Jewish businesses. Fired up, the congregation acted
on his advice at once.

The threat of violence simmered, but it didn't boil over among
the mobs who left the church that day and passed the street on
which most of the city's Jews lived. However, for those people who

might have had either a first-hand or a folk memory of the Russian pogroms, their fear was very real.

After a week during which there was much tension, and occasional close calls for Jewish businesses and their owners themselves, Creagh returned to the pulpit. He had not softened his attitude in the meantime. While asking that there be no violence against the city's Jewish population, he once again proved himself to be an expert rabble-rouser: 'If the Jews are allowed to go on as they have been doing,' he told the congregation, 'in a short time we will be their absolute slaves, and slavery to them is worse than slavery to which Cromwell condemned the poor Irish who were shipped to the Barbadoes.'

He concluded: 'Let us defend ourselves before their heels are too firmly planted upon our necks.'

The boycott became world news. On 12 April 1904, the *New York Times* reported that:

> . . . if a correspondent of *The London Times* is to be believed, there exists in Limerick a state of affairs paralleled only in the darkest parts of 'Holy Russia' . . . According to this surprising letter, the thirty-five Jewish families living in Limerick have been made the objects of a boycott so relentless that all of them, with one or two exceptions, are ruined, and many are on the verge of starvation.

As the boycott continued, some Jewish children were refused service in shops. In April a 15-year-old boy was sentenced to a month in jail for throwing stones at three Jews, including Limerick's rabbi. Creagh found himself championed by many, including Arthur Griffiths' *United Irishman*, which wrote: 'We have no quarrel with the Jews' religion; but all the howling of journalistic hacks and balderdash of uninformed sentimentalists will not make us, nor should it make any honest man, cease to expose knavery, because knavery is carried on by Jews.'

Not everyone agreed with Father Creagh's assessment. One letter sent to him read. 'So you low cur—had you nothing better to tell your people than to set them on the poor unfortunate Jews? You call yourself a Minister of God. You are a minister of the Devil. You are a disgrace to the Catholic religion, you brute.'

Amidst the excited comment, there were those who were prepared to point out that for the Irish to accuse anyone else of dishonesty would be a touch hypocritical. Standish Hayes O'Grady, editor of the *All-Ireland Review*, wrote that:

> The Jews have not taught us these vile tricks and dishonest shortcuts to wealth; we had them and practised them all along before he came, and we are at them still, and would be at them were we to expel the whole race of Jews en masse tomorrow. If there were no Jews in Ireland, our own Christian usurers . . . would do just the same bad work, only without competition.

At this remove, it appears a strange line of defence for the Jewish population—they do bad work, but the Irish already do it themselves—but it would have been welcomed by them nonetheless, because their businessmen did suffer badly in Limerick.

One of them, Marcus Joseph Blond, wrote to the press in April 1904.

> It took me all these years, with the greatest pain and trouble and working unceasingly until I established myself comfortably and enjoyed a nice trade, until, all of a sudden, like a thunderstorm, spoke hatred and animosity against the Jews, how they crucified Lord Jesus, how they martyred St Simon, and gradually in one month's time, I have none of my previous customers coming into my shop. In fact, my business is nil at present, would you call my trade a national evil?

Blond took to placing press advertisements that read: 'MJ Blond, 60 Henry Street. Whose trade has been practically ruined, by the recent agitation, earnestly begs the support of his Protestant friends and customers and promises every attention to their wants.'

In all, the boycott lasted two years. The event became known as the Limerick Pogrom, although that somewhat exaggerated the distressing, but not bloody, events that occurred in the city that year. Still, it had an impact on the small community. By March 1905, it was officially estimated that five families had left Limerick because of the 'agitation', although the community's own statistics claimed that 70 rather than 32 people had departed.

As for Creagh, he was sent on missionary work in the Philippines in 1906, having first been waved off by a large crowd at Limerick's railway station. He later moved on to Australia and then New Zealand, eventually dying in 1947 in a Wellington hospital.

The year the Limerick boycott began, 1904, was also the year in which *Ulysses* was set, in which Joyce gave Ireland not only one of its most famous fictional characters, Leopold Bloom, but arguably its most famous Jew. Joyce used Bloom as an archetypal outsider and wanderer, who saw himself as Irish even if others kept emphasising his difference. Through him, he allows another character the ironic quip that the Irish had never persecuted the Jews, because 'We never let them in.'

That wasn't true, of course. In fact, as the Litvak and Irish neighbourhoods mingled, Ó Gráda says that 'for most of their existence these Litvak-Irish neighbourhoods were successful experiments in multiculturalism'. Still, that line from *Ulysses* would come to have a tragic resonance in the 1930s when the rise of Hitler led to a growing Jewish refugee crisis across Europe as families were forced out of Germany and Austria. The Irish government proved generally unsympathetic to their plight.

In the pre-war years applications for refuge went through one man: the Irish Ambassador to Germany, Charles Bewley. He really did not like Jews at all. He made this clear in one message to the Taoiseach at the time, Eamon de Valera, informing him that 'Jewish emigrants in the countries which they have been permitted to enter have created and are creating grave moral scandals and are a source of corruption of the populations among which they dwell'.

Bewley was not a maverick voice in this regard, with Department of Justice representatives later admitting that they were tighter on applications from Jews than they were on others. Bewley was replaced in 1939, but with the outbreak of war attitudes continued to harden. Even towards the end of 1945, a memorandum on the Admission of Aliens explained: 'It is the policy of the Department of Justice to restrict the immigration of Jews . . . As Jews do not become assimilated . . . there is a danger that any big increase in their numbers might create a social problem.'

Unusual laws were enacted during the period, notably an Act of 1936 that stated 'it shall not be lawful for any alien . . . to assume or use . . . any name other than the name by which he was ordinarily and usually known' without a licence to do so. Some had done so in order to blend in more easily.

In 1939, there were 2,610 'aliens' registered in Ireland, 1,297 of whom were Americans. There were 326 Germans, while the rest included small numbers of Russians, Belgians, Czechoslovaks, Polish, Argentines and six 'Iraquian'. And that year, as war broke out in Europe, only 292 migrants were admitted into Ireland. That was still more than were to be accepted in total between then and the end of the war in 1945.

Before the war even broke out 147,000 of Austria's 206,000 Jews went into exile. Of these, 27,000 went as far as Great Britain, so the numbers arriving in Ireland were very small. When, in 1938, the Cork Jewish Refugees Committee announced that Jewish refugees were to come to Ireland, they went out of their way to reassure the natives that there would be conditions, including that they were to be only temporary settlers and that the Jewish community should bear the full cost rather than expect the taxpayer to do so. Those Jewish adults who were to work here were not to earn a wage through jobs that might otherwise go to Irish citizens.

An Irish Co-ordinating Committee for Refugees was formed to assess applications, with the final go-ahead going to the Minister for Justice. They were allowed three categories: 50 workers from a group of agricultural workers trained by the Quakers; adults already with sponsorship and who would be emigrating onwards; and children who were also expected to move on once educated. They were not to allow 'doctors, dentists and other professional men as it would be highly undesirable to permit foreign doctors to practise in this country'.

During the war, the attitude to the Jews was not helped by the imposition of a media censorship that was mainly to ensure neutral Ireland wasn't seen to be taking sides. Some newspaper editors found ingenious ways around it, such as the pictures on the front page of the *Irish Times* on the day the war in Europe ended which formed a V for victory. But the censorship had the result of keeping out news of the suffering of the Jewish populations under the Third Reich. The British were regularly given such information for news and propaganda purposes, but Irish were newspapers and newsreels were stripped of much of the horror, perhaps preventing people here from developing a sympathy that would have possibly encouraged the young State to become more welcoming of victims.

Nevertheless, in 1943 Eamon de Valera agreed to accept 500 refugee children from Vichy France, although the Red Cross— which was to bring them—consented to omit the word 'Jewish' from their reports. De Valera was not unsympathetic to the Jewish community in Ireland, but it seems that there were others who were. This was borne out when a plan to bring 100 Jewish children from the Bergen-Belsen refugee camp was restricted by the Minister for Justice on the basis that it was always policy to restrict Jewish aliens from coming into Ireland. When the Chief

Rabbi appealed to de Valera, the Taoiseach intervened and allowed them in. But only temporarily. The 100 children were soon relocated to Britain, Canada, Israel and the US.

Five children were brought independently from Bergen-Belsen following the war by an Irish Red Cross volunteer, Robert Collis, and his future wife Han (a Dutch nurse) and were subsequently adopted by Robert and Han and two other Dublin couples.

In the post-war years, Dublin's Jewish population fragmented, some emigrating to the US or Israel, and others drifting towards the suburbs so leading to the decline of Little Jerusalem and the closure of the synagogues. It said much for how quickly they had ceased to become one of the larger ethnic communities in Ireland when some mild controversy followed the decision in 2006 to remove the box on the census form that allowed a person to specify themselves as Jewish. They are now in the 'other' category. It was an inevitable result of the community's decline. The 2002 census had put their numbers in the Republic at 1,790, or less than 1 per cent of the population. This was less than half its peak of 3,907 in 1946.

By 2006, the Jewish population in Ireland had risen slightly, a by-product of the large inward migration in the intervening years, but there were three times as many Hindus in Ireland, several thousand more Jehovah's Witnesses. There were only marginally more Jews than there were Pantheists. And there were 32,000 Muslims. The irony was that a great many of them had settled around Portobello, the area once known as Little Jerusalem.

Chapter 7 ∽

188 AND COUNTING: THE RECENT ARRIVALS

Towards the end of the 1990s, a person could have made a few predictions about Gort in Co. Galway. But none of them, it's fair to say, would have involved a Samba festival and the local Abrakebabra burger joint sitting next to a Brazilian shop that stocked palm hearts and pinto beans. They would not have featured Brazilian music nights in the local pubs. And any crystal ball gazing would have been seen as pretty cracked if it had suggested that within five years a third of the population of this small Galway town would have been born in a place several thousand miles away on the edge of a South American city.

But there it is, this Irish village on the edge of the Burren that has become an extended suburb of a city in central Brazil. If there was ever a statistic that so completely captured the suddenness, the extent and the occasional surrealism of the immigration into Ireland at the turn of the twenty-first century, it is this one.

On one level, the Brazilians' arrival in the town shouldn't really have seemed so surprising. In a roaring Irish economy, their skills were sought by a meat industry that was struggling with a labour shortage. The Brazilians had lost their jobs when their local meat factory had closed down; meat workers were needed in Ireland. It was a simple equation, needing only for someone to make the connection and set the whole thing in train.

But the appearance over the course of just a few years of almost a thousand South Americans in a corner of Ireland from which people had historically emigrated had a quirkiness that proved irresistible to the world's media. The *New York Times* paid the town a visit. German television made a documentary.

It had all begun with the closure of a meat factory in the town of Vila Fabril, a suburb of Anápolis in central Brazil, and a place surrounded by coffee plantations and fields of soy and bananas. The collapse of the industry in the mid-1990s put 900 local men and women out of work. This included at least one man who was not so local at all. An Irishman who had been a manager at the factory arranged for 25 of its ex-workers to take jobs in a factory in Clonee, Co. Meath. Soon, other meat processors began to source workers from Vila Fabril and, in 1999, Sean Duffy Meat Exports Ltd of Gort brought six Brazilians to the town.

These turned out to be pioneers. Within a few years, the path would be so well trodden that the money being sent home from Ireland was visible in the renovated and brightly coloured houses of Vila Fabril and the inhabitants began to refer to Ireland as Fabril 2. In Gort, they nicknamed their town 'Little Brazil'.

Over two censuses, Gort was one of the fastest growing towns on an island in which there was plenty of competition. Its population jumped 50 per cent each time. Although Brazilians were not the only foreigners among the 2,646 people living in the town in 2006, they made up the vast majority of the 40 per cent of Gort's population that had not been born in Ireland.

The thing about Gort is that it is exceptional in one way, but unexceptional in others. In almost every large town in Ireland after 1995 there were demographic changes of a sort few could have predicted. No one would have guessed that one of the country's last surviving Butlins camps, Mosney in Co. Meath, would become a reception centre for asylum seekers from dozens of countries. No one would have foreseen that Moore Street, one of the great symbols of Dublin and its people, would be revitalised by its transformation into an ethnic shopping street, with Asian markets and African hairdressers. No one would have guessed in

1994, a year of net emigration, that a decade later one out of every 10 people living in Ireland would have been born in another country.

And then, in keeping with a trend that seemed only to confirm the futility of guessing what the next trend would be, things changed again. In 2009, as the country was firmly in recession, the newspaper headlines began focussing again on the outflow, on a return to emigration by those born in Ireland, and a return home for those who had come here during the boom years. It meant that, when it came to migration, Ireland's graph was sharper than a shark's teeth. Huge outflows were followed by massive inflows. There were sudden reversals of trends and just when the country was getting used to the graph going in one direction, it would sharply veer in the other.

It was easy to see why, in 2007, the *Irish Times*'s recently appointed Migration Correspondent Ruadhán Mac Cormaic wrote that: 'So fluid and fast-moving are the changes being wrought here by immigration that writing about it can feel like photographing a moving train at night, the result a streaky blur that, however elegant at first glance, will be of no use to anyone in the morning.'

———

On a night in April 1996, a census was held across the Republic of Ireland. When the statisticians began to trawl through the figures, a surprising result emerged. Although the increase in births over deaths was at its lowest for half a century, in the five years since the previous census, the population had jumped. In itself, this wasn't a shock. The population of Ireland had gone up in every census bar one since the 1960s. Even though the exception to that had come in the previous census of 1991, at the height of emigration from Ireland, the statisticians knew that there had been a recovery. They just hadn't realised how healthy it had been.

Once the 1996 figures were tallied, it was realised that there were 30,000 more people in the country than had been predicted. This meant that the population was almost 1 per cent higher than previously presumed. That mightn't seem like much, but being ambushed by even a single percentage point can make it tricky to plan the future of a country's infrastructure. And those extra people were an indication that something major was about to happen.

In fact 1996 was the year in which Ireland finally stopped being a country from which people left and instead became one of net immigration. It was the last EU country of the 15 at the time to reach that milestone. It was not, though, the first year of net immigration in the country's recent history.

The entire 1970s were years in which more people came into Ireland than left it. There were even some similarities with the immigration of the 1990s. Spurred by an upswing in the country's economic fortunes, many of the Irish who had previously emigrated took their chance to come home again, bringing their families with them. And just as happened in the 1990s, by doing so they helped Ireland go from being the European country with the highest rate of emigration to one of net immigration in the space of just a decade.

The census of 1979 gives us some good statistics on all of this. It even contrives to give us a glimpse of the morality of the time because in the question on a person's marital status, people were given the options of confirming that they were single, married, widowed or 'other'—7,624 people classified themselves as other. In the final tally, these 'others' were just lumped into the married category anyway.

More pertinently, it confirmed that 109,000 more people came into Ireland than had left it during the 1970s. There was a significant caveat, though. Many of those who immigrated were actually older returned emigrants and there was still a net outflow of Irish under the age of 25. Even so, this spell of immigration had quite an effect on the country's demographics. The population of the country jumped by over 13 per cent in just 10 years.

Of course, in historical terms, the 1970s could be treated as a blip compared with what happened before or after it. Or it could be seen as a very early taster of what was to come a couple of decades later. Either side of it, the trend had been firmly towards an outflow of people. At times Ireland was a European leader in the field.

As the 1970s ended, Ireland was quickly reverting to type. Huge numbers left until emigration from Ireland peaked in 1989, when about 44,000 more people left the country than entered it. In all, about 70,000 people departed our shores that year, one in 50 of the population at the time. In isolation, perhaps that figure doesn't even sound too drastic, but added up over the previous 10 years it amounted to a lot of Irish leaving for work abroad. Enough, in fact, for there to be a drop in the overall population of Ireland at the end of the 1980s—the first decline since the end of the nineteenth century.

The thing about it, though, is that emigration didn't just fizzle out, it shuddered to an almost complete halt in only a few years. Remember that emigration *peaked* in 1989 and yet Ireland became an immigrant nation in only half a decade. This was such a novelty that there were serious concerns expressed at the time that this amount of immigration coupled with a global recession could cause unemployment to jump to 300,000. As it happened, the economy was about to take off with such force that half a million jobs were created between 1991 and 2001 and the country's labour force expanded by 43 per cent. There were hardly enough people to feed the demand for an economy that had effectively created full employment and complaints that there weren't enough people coming in to fill the jobs.

Throughout the late 1990s and into the 2000s, a significant proportion of immigrants to Ireland were returned Irish. Between 1995 and 2000, there were over 120,000 of them in all. That they comprised half of arrivals gives a clear idea of just how many people were coming into Ireland at the time. It was to have a huge effect on the counties whose populations had once been decimated by emigration. For example, Leitrim, whose population had plummeted since the Famine, suddenly found itself gaining people for the first time in many decades.

By April 2002, of the 644,400 people who were treated as long-term migrants living in Ireland, 366,800 were returned Irish emigrants. And a quarter of a million of them had come home at some time during the previous six years.

Actually, the phenomenon of the returned emigrant wasn't completely new, globally or to Ireland. It has always been a trend within global migration, even during times when to our perspective it seems unlikely. In the nineteenth century maybe a quarter of all the people who left Europe for America are thought to have returned. This figure is borne out by steamship statistics from between 1897 and 1907, which showed that a third of those who had emigrated from Europe had actually gone back home again.

Ireland's experience was never quite on that scale, but it is still estimated that about a tenth of all the people who left its shores for America during the 1800s eventually returned. It certainly makes sense that at particular times in an economic cycle, people who have moved somewhere in the hope of a job cut their losses and return home when employment dries up. During the Great Depression year of 1931, the United States said goodbye to twice as many migrants as it welcomed. And in 1932, 10 times as many people moved from America to Ireland as went in the other direction. To be fair, that figure is not as startling as it might at first sound, because only 256 Irish are recorded as having left for the States in the first place. But it still gives us a good idea of what was going on at the time and challenges the popular belief that the flow of human traffic had been in one direction only.

As we've seen in the previous chapters, immigration wasn't exactly unknown in Ireland. And even at a time when Ireland was cementing its place as the European country with the highest rate of emigration, there had been a trickle of people coming into the country. Apart from the programme refugees, there were the economic migrants, such as the Italians. And from the 1950s on, there was a small but growing Muslim population that—with a certain irony that has not gone unnoticed—began to settle around the area of Dublin previously known as Little Jerusalem.

Why the Muslim population gravitated towards the Jewish area is a little unclear. It has been speculated that the newcomers ate kosher meat before halal was available in the city (the first halal butcher came to Ireland in 1975, the year Dublin's first mosque opened). It has also been suggested that it was simply down to the practicality of the area being close to the College of Surgeons, which had attracted Muslim students to Dublin since the mid-1950s. However, by the 1991 census, their numbers were still relatively small—fewer than 4,000 across the Republic.

And there had always been a flow of people from across the Irish Sea. The 1996 census confirmed that of all the foreign-born people in Ireland, 72 per cent were British. To be more precise, it told us that 66 per cent were from England and Wales and that 6 per cent were Scottish. After them, Americans were the next best-represented foreigners on the island, accounting for 7 per cent.

But few were particularly interested in those statistics, because at that stage it was becoming clear that Ireland was increasingly attractive not just to British or returning Irish but to people for whom the last island on the way out of western Europe must have seemed like the end of the earth.

————

In 2001, Karede Guler and his wife Saniye, and their two children, nine-year-old Imam and four-year-old Berkan, left their home in the Kurdish region of Turkey. They had sold everything they owned to scrape together the £25,000 it cost to be smuggled to what they hoped would be a better life in Britain. First, they flew from Istanbul to Sarajevo (which required no visa), then travelled by truck and train, north across Europe, through Austria and Germany until they finally arrived in Brussels.

There they met with Kadriye Kalendergil and her husband Hasan, who had a 16-year-old son, Kalender, and 10-year-old daughter, Zehila. Hasan had been a farmer in south-east Turkey, but had left to work as a street trader in Istanbul, claiming to have been forced out by the Turkish military's fight against Kurdish separatists. His support for the Kurdish movement led to him being jailed in Istanbul, after which he decided to take his family to Britain and claim asylum. Their route to Brussels also took them first to Sarajevo, but then on through Switzerland to Paris, where they took a train to Belgium.

The families were all put up in a hotel in Brussels used by their smugglers, where they were joined by three other Turkish Kurds, an Algerian and an Albanian—all male. Each had paid about £5,000 to be taken to Britain. On the cold, wet night of 3 December they gathered at a petrol station on the edge of Brussels, where they were to begin the final leg of their journey.

Their smugglers told them to climb into the compartment of a truck that was carrying furniture. They were told that they would be going through the southern English port of Dover and that the journey would take only a few hours. One of their smugglers gave them bottles of mineral water and some cheese to sustain them on their journey, and asked them to double-check the destination of the furniture packed in beside them. It was confirmed that a label read 'Luton/London'. Then the door was shut and its security seal layered with silicone gel.

The truck's driver did not know that he was carrying human cargo. And what neither the Kalendergils, Gulers, their fellow passengers or even their smugglers knew was that the truck was not on its way to Dover. Instead, a change of plan had meant that the furniture would go direct to Wexford instead of being sent through a Luton warehouse as it normally was.

By the time the vehicle was driven onto a ferry at Zeebrugge, the 13 migrants had already been in the hold for 15 hours. Once onboard, they remained trapped in the truck's container, which was parked in the ship's hold, beside the ship's hot engine. They had no light or ventilation. The ferry sailed into a force 10 gale. When they finally reached Ireland, their journey of 'hours' had taken days.

When they arrived in Wexford, the wrong container was sent to the business park where the furniture was supposed to go. It was a full day before the mistake was realised and their box was located. By the time the doors were finally opened, the container had been sealed shut for 100 hours. It had become a coffin. The two Guler children were dead, as was their mother. Their father Karede was just about alive. Kadriye Kalendergil's husband and two children were dead, although she had survived. In all, eight of the passengers had died. The other two were Yuksel Ucaroglu and Mostafa Demir.

In 2003, seven men—but not the truck's driver—were convicted in a Bruges court for their role in the human smuggling ring that led to the deaths. Failed asylum seekers themselves, they received sentences of between two and 10 years, although the ringleaders were sentenced in their absence and have never been caught. It was estimated by the prosecutor that the gang had earned an annual income of €12 million through smuggling 200 people a month into Britain.

That the refugees were not originally destined for Ireland doesn't matter. Their experience was a terrible reminder of how Ireland had become a node in the human smuggling network in a way that it had never experienced before. Although, we already knew that. What this dreadful event really showed was the lengths people would go to in order to seek a better life in a richer country.

——

The story of Ireland's recent immigrations can arguably be split into two parts: a first wave which came before 2004, and a second that came from eastern Europe after the expansions of the EU in 2004 and 2007. And although they were not the bulk of the immigrants during the earliest part of this, the number of asylum seekers who suddenly turned up in Ireland was something that hadn't been anticipated, and which somehow became emblematic of the way the country's demographics were being altered so quickly and visibly.

As we've already seen, there had been refugee programmes before, and in 1999, over a thousand Kosovars were brought to Ireland during the conflict there, although this was only considered to be 'temporary protection', and the following year most of them went home again (only 150 decided to stay on in Ireland).

Unexpected asylum seekers, though, were hardly a factor at the beginning of the 1990s, when only about 50 people sought refuge in Ireland each year. When you consider that across Europe as a whole in 1990 there were 400,000 asylum seekers, this was beyond minuscule compared with the numbers experienced by our neighbours. In 1992, in fact, there were a mere 36 applications for asylum in Ireland. It would not be so low again. As the decade progressed, the numbers climbed steeply until 2002, when over 11,500 people arrived in Ireland in search of asylum.

While asylum seekers were at first living mostly in the greater Dublin area, a policy of dispersal was then carried out, through which they were spread around the country. As the numbers seeking asylum rose, the Irish government examined various options. In 2000, it considered housing them in prefabricated pods on land at Dublin airport, and that same year the idea of 'floating hotels' (or 'flotels') was also mooted and investigated through a government trip to a similar facility in the Netherlands. The idea was soon sunk.

Among them was Mosney, on the sliver of Meath coastline that separates Dublin from Louth. It had been built as a holiday camp in 1948—the first Butlins outside Britain—and during its heyday welcomed 2,800 campers to its chalets and 4,000 daytrippers. By the time Butlins sold the camp to a new operator in 1982, the era of the foreign sun holiday had already sent business on an irreversible decline. That Mosney survived as a holiday camp into the twenty-first century made it something of an anomaly, but in 2000 it had its last season, its train station was closed and that, it appeared, was that.

Until, in that same year, its owners signed a new deal with the Department of Justice which would make Mosney the country's largest accommodation centre for asylum seekers, a holding place for 800 people who could not work while waiting for their applications to be accepted or declined. It became a bizarre waiting area for people from over 50 countries, who took up residence in the strips of chalet blocks, ate in the restaurants that once fed holidaying Irish families and dipped in the swimming pool with its mushroom waterfalls.

By 2005, it was one of 63 accommodation centres across Ireland—some purpose built, others pre-existing hostels—which housed over 6,000 asylum seekers. Mosney was the main holding camp on the east coast, and yet it was tucked away off the road, along its own stretch of coast, so that the only idea any passing motorist might have that there was an asylum seekers' camp nearby was the sight of so many foreigners waiting at the bus stop.

Yet, by then the numbers were already dropping and centres were closing. There had been two significant changes in the law: the first had come in 2003, when the Supreme Court ruled that parents of children born in Ireland were no longer automatically entitled to become Irish citizens. And a constitutional referendum in June 2004 compounded that ruling when the electorate voted by a four-to-one majority to remove the right of any child born in Ireland to become an Irish citizen. It had been the only EU country to allow that in the first place.

The Minister for Justice at the time, Michael McDowell, had

claimed in advance of that referendum that up to half of foreign-born women who were giving birth in Irish maternity hospitals did so in order to attain Irish citizenship for their children. The government described those as 'citizenship tourists'. The masters of the maternity hospitals had indeed expressed their concerns over the number of foreign women arriving in hospitals (sometimes showing up for the first time when in labour) and they warned that this was putting pressure on services. Of the 22,895 births in Dublin's three maternity hospitals the previous year, 4,400 had been to non-EU nationals.

Since then the number of asylum seekers has dropped markedly. In 2008, 3,866 applied for asylum in the Republic, which was less than a third of the peak figure. The five countries from which asylum seekers were most likely to come were Nigeria, Pakistan, Iraq, Georgia and China. Since 2000, Nigerians have accounted for between 30 and 40 per cent of applications for asylum.

And yet, the State could keep track of statistics, but found it a lot harder to keep track of people. At the close of 2008, the government admitted that it had lost a total of 400 immigrant children who had arrived in Ireland unaccompanied by an adult.

———

For all the attention that they received, the asylum seekers—successful and unsuccessful—were only a small proportion of the overall numbers who came to Ireland from the mid-1990s onwards. But the number of people coming from outside the EU was increasing to the point where between 2000 and 2003 returned Irish no longer made up the bulk of migrants (they were now just over 40 per cent). During that time, about 100,000 people from outside the EU were granted work visas, which meant that by 2002, roughly 2 per cent of the Irish population was from outside the EU.

The change happened so rapidly that neither Ireland nor the countries from which the migrants came had much time to prepare for it. It led to some unusual situations. The Filipino community in Ireland, for instance, consists chiefly of nurses— seven out of 10 female Filipinos living in Ireland worked in the health system—because their country remains the largest exporter of registered nurses in the world. They often travel to Ireland without their families but send money home, contributing to the €15 billion that Filipinos all around the world send home every year.

During the early 2000s on Wednesday and Saturday nights, Dublin's main bus station, Busáras, became an improvised Filipino embassy, with business conducted at a table in the terminal's main waiting area. An average of 80 people a night would travel from various towns across the island in search of advice, help, forms and newspapers from home.

However swiftly things had changed until that point, they were about to accelerate even more. In 2004, the EU welcomed 10 new states as members. Crucially, Ireland had joined only Britain and Sweden in automatically allowing citizens of those first 10 countries full working rights, at a time when other EU countries had decided to delay that privilege. By the time that Romania and Bulgaria joined in 2007, the attitude had hardened somewhat, with their citizens having to apply for employment visas. But by then, the impact of EU enlargement had already been enormous. Ireland had experienced a fresh surge of immigration that utterly changed the demographics. By 2006, Polish was unofficially the second language of the Republic of Ireland. More people spoke it on a daily basis than spoke Irish.

This could be considered to be something of a surprise, not least because as recently as 2002 Ireland had no direct flights to Poland. Within a few years, it not only had several direct flights, it even had a direct bus that left from Dublin's quays, boarded a ferry to England, picked up passengers in Manchester,

Birmingham and London, travelled on through the Netherlands and Germany, and then began its stops in Poznań, Łódź and Warsaw, where those passengers who had been on it since the very beginning disembarked, their legs half-seized up after a 42-hour journey. Then the bus would turn around and start the return journey.

By then, though, things which would have seemed somewhat outlandish even a short time before were part of everyday life. Even in small towns across Ireland it had become easy enough to find eastern European shops, halal meat and cheap telephone kiosks. There were radio stations for immigrants. In 2002, there were five African newspapers and magazines printed in Ireland. There were Polish newspapers and Dublin's only evening paper, the *Evening Herald*, printed a Polish section each week. At a time of declining attendances at churches across Ireland, about 100 African churches opened up in less than a decade. In the 2009 local elections, over 40 immigrant candidates were on the ballot papers and they battled for a share of foreign nationals' votes with the aid of multilingual websites and leaflets as well as full-time political organisers from the migrant communities.

The most detailed attempt yet to capture the fluid population was taken in the census of the night of 23 April 2006. It says something about the state of the nation that it was only the second time a straight nationality question had been asked on the census form.

This time around the form was available in 11 languages other than English and Irish. These included Chinese, Arabic, Romanian and Portuguese, although an information leaflet was printed in several more languages including Yoruba, which is spoken in Nigeria and other west African countries.

And among the four new questions on the form was Question 14, which asked: 'What is your ethnic or cultural background?'

By the time the results of the 2006 census were published, there was no longer any real surprise about the scale of change, only curiosity about the details. Over 120,000 of the people who filled in the form had not been living in Ireland 12 months before. Of a population of over 4.2 million, it emerged that 419,733 were not Irish. On that night in Ireland, there were 63,000 Poles and 24,500 Lithuanians. There were over 35,000 Africans, 16,000 of whom were Nigerian. There were also, officially at least, 11,000 Chinese and 4,388 Brazilians.

For whatever reason, 45,597 people did not state their nationality. But we do know that there were representatives of 188 nations in Ireland on that date. There were citizens of Belize, Bhutan, Burma, Bermuda and Benin. There were people from Macao and Turkmenistan and Iraq.

There was at least one person from Niue, a Polynesian island one of whose principal sources of income include selling its stamps to foreign collectors, although it has also been described as one of the world's leading money-laundering spots. Niue has suffered badly due to emigration over recent decades, with many going to New Zealand, the protectorate state of which Niue's people are actually citizens. At the last count, the island had a population of 1,444. It would have been 1,445 if at least one of them hadn't ended up in Ireland for whatever reason.

The census results went into almost unnecessary, but nonetheless often delightful, detail. For instance, of the 165 towns in Ireland, only 28 had no Chinese residents, even though two-thirds of the Chinese population lives in Dublin. A quarter of these Chinese were homemakers; 10 per cent of them were retired; their average age was 26.9 years; 2 per cent of Chinese men and 7 per cent of women lived with an Irish partner; 80 per cent of them had no religion (this made them the most godless nationality on the island). Really, it was just short of telling us that 13 per cent of them had porridge for their breakfast.

Some other statistics to emerge from the 2006 census included the fact that the Polish had the most lopsided gender gap, with two-thirds of their migrants being men. Only nine towns in all of

Ireland had no Lithuanians among the population. Less than 1 per cent of Nigerians had 'no religion'. Nearly half of Nigerian children could speak Irish. Eight per cent of the Americans in Ireland were disabled.

Even then, there was some cynicism expressed about the accuracy of the census. There were claims—albeit unsupported—that there were 30,000 Chinese in Ireland, which was three times the official statistic; and there may have been four times the 4,720 Brazilians who were officially counted.

Nevertheless, once again the largely overlooked statistic was how no other nationality came even close to matching the size of the biggest ethnic group outside the Irish. In 2006, there were 120,000 British living in Ireland, an increase of 9 per cent on the previous census figure. Just over half of those identified as English were likely to live in a rural area. Cork was the most popular county for them, with almost one in ten of Kinsale's population being English. They were also the oldest immigrants, with an average age of 38.7. One in six of them was retired. And giving us some idea of their motivation for moving west, 17 per cent of them actually identified their ethnic or cultural background as being 'Irish'.

The census report which delves into these statistics has a picture of a man in an English soccer jersey hugging a young boy who is wearing a Manchester United shirt and a furry, tricoloured Viking hat. Clearly, the man didn't buy his shirt in the Republic of Ireland, because for all that has changed in the relationship between the two countries in recent years, you are still more likely to walk into a sports shop and pick up a Niue soccer jersey than an English one.

Quite what all these non-Irish were supposed to be called was itself a source of a little angst over the years. For some time, the standard euphemism was 'non-national', a phrase which clearly made little sense given that almost everyone arriving in Ireland (or any other land) is of some nationality. There were even rare occasions when the nonsensical 'non-national Irish' was used. It has since become increasingly unacceptable as a phrase, partly because it was thought that it could be misinterpreted as relating to asylum seekers.

In 2006, the Department of Justice decided to review its use in official documents, although this came only eight years after it had stopped using its previous legal term for non-Irish: 'alien'. In fact, while introducing the term 'non-national' to the Immigration Bill of 1999, the Minister for Justice at the time, John O'Donoghue, had remarked: 'This expression is more in keeping with modern usage than the term "alien", which has been used in the Aliens Act 1935. Nowadays it is more likely to conjure up images of outer space than of people from other countries. I am happier to see its use discontinued.'

This linguistic conundrum, it's worth observing, wasn't a uniquely Irish concern. In 2005, the Prime Minister of Antigua and Barbuda announced that other Caribbean islanders shouldn't be referred to as non-nationals. 'Non-native' became the islands' term of choice.

In Ireland, 'non-national' ran concurrently with the term 'The New Irish', which itself caused a certain amount of controversy, with the objections to it including the rather straightforward observation that any Irish person who moved to London would not be happy to be referred to as one of the 'New English'.

In the 2006 census there was also the debut of that question about ethnic background. The results, for what it is worth, showed that 95 per cent of the population were of a 'white back-ground', 1.3 per cent were Asian or Asian-Irish and 1 per cent were Black or Black Irish. It didn't reveal much about immigration as such, because a person's ethnic background doesn't tell you anything about where they were born, but the statistic is worth mentioning nonetheless. (More recent statistics point up to the longer-term impact on the population: the numbers with 'black ethnicity' grow the younger the demographic until it is 3 per cent for 0–4-year-olds. In all, 15 per cent of 0–4-year-olds in Ireland are currently of non-Irish ethnicity.)

At that point, we knew that a total of 840,000 adult immigrants had been admitted into the Republic over the previous six years. It was a staggering figure, although it's important to note that they didn't all stay. Only half of them were still working six years later, many of the rest presumably having left.

As ever, the statisticians could dazzle with details. Of those 423,000 still working in Ireland by the end of 2007, most were men (256,000 of them compared with 167,000 women). This is another of the many differences between the immigration of the 2000s compared with that of the 1970s. Back then a small majority of immigrants—most of them returned emigrants, remember— were women.

What did this do to the population? In 1996, there were 3,626,087 people in the Republic of Ireland. By 2002, when the next census was taken (it had been postponed for a year by an outbreak of foot-and-mouth disease), the population had gone up to 3,917,203, an increase of over 7 per cent in six years. The population then jumped a further 8 per cent to 4,239,848 by 2006.

Immigration had been responsible for nearly two-thirds of the population increase: 48 per cent of the migrants had come from the 12 new European Union member states. For a country whose population had actually declined in 1991, and which had been surprised by a rise of only 100,000 in the five years after that, this had been a turnaround of near-exceptional proportions. Not since the Plantations had there been such an influx of people into the island of Ireland.

What might make the 2006 census increasingly important is that it may well have been taken in the same year in which Ireland hit its high point as a place of net immigration: 71,800 more people came into the country than left it in the year ending April 2006. It didn't mean that immigration stopped straight after it. Far from it, in fact. In the year ending April 2007, a record number of migrants entered Ireland. A total of 109,500 came and half of them were from the countries of eastern Europe. Almost 80,000 Poles came to Ireland, or at least this was the number that applied for public personal service numbers, which are required for employment or to access social services. (Curiously, 4,000 people from Mauritius applied for those numbers too.) But there was now an increased outflow too. Net immigration was down to 67,000 in that year.

It was the beginning of a trend. By the end of 2008, there had been a growth in the numbers of migrants looking for help to repatriate. The International Organisation for Migration, using funding given to them by the EU and the Irish government, would give up to €400 per person (or €1,200 per family) to help asylum seekers and undocumented migrants pay for a flight home. In 2007, 250 people had applied for that assistance. Moldovans and Georgians featured prominently on the list of the 30 nationalities applying, but those most likely to look for help were Brazilians. By 2008, they made up almost half of all applicants.

In April 2007, Sean Duffy's meat factory in Gort had closed. The previous year, a fire had extensively damaged the building, without injury to any of the workers. But the closure of the factory that had brought the first Brazilians to Gort, and then kept them coming, seemed to mark a turn in the relationship between a shantytown in Brazil and a once monochrome Irish village.

In 2008, Ireland remained top of the European immigration league, on a percentage basis anyway. In that same report, Ireland was confirmed as having the highest birth rate and the lowest death rate in the EU. Yet, by late 2008, the Central Statistics Office was forecasting that Dublin's population would fall for the first time since the Famine if immigrants stopped coming. It estimated that the population of the city would fall by 100,000 even if immigration and emigration balanced out.

Of all the jobs created in Ireland in 2008, 90 per cent were taken by non-Irish workers. Yet, in just one week, as the recession began to bite, the numbers of non-Irish signing on the dole jumped a full 100 per cent from 16,000 to 32,000.

All of which made predicting what would happen next an inexact science to say the least. It had become such a variable that the guesswork about just how many people could end up living in Ireland had to leave itself enormous room for manoeuvre. Official estimates as to what the population will be by 2041 are unsurprisingly varied. Depending on a number of factors—chief among them being the amount of immigration—there could be 7.1 million living in the Republic or there may be just 4.9 million. Irrespective of immigration trends, between 1.3 million and 1.4 million of those will be aged over 65, although the average life expectancy is estimated to be 86 for men and 88 for women by then.

It seems only reasonable that Ireland should hedge its bets on this subject. In 2004, the Central Statistics Office had claimed that the country would need 50,000 immigrants a year for the following 12 years in order to sustain the current economic growth. At that point, the net immigration was 30,000 (50,000 coming in, but 20,000 going out). And they got their numbers for a few years after that. But five years later, the economy was on its knees. And people were talking about a return to net emigration.

———

In 1986, the *Irish Times* looked at a new phenomenon of Irish life. 'Rice, pasta and salami,' it reported, 'are replacing bacon and potatoes in many Irish shopping baskets.'

It continued: 'It is arguable that ethnic cooking has penetrated all social classes, in both town and country, to varying degrees.' Of a total of 498 restaurants in Ireland, 124 of these were ethnic eateries, which the article classified as meaning 'Greek, Chinese, Italian'.

Readers learned that:

. . . the kiwi has already arrived in Moore Street and is doing very well. Vera, who has had a stand on the street for 30 years and describes herself as the 'third generation of a Moore Street dynasty', says it is simply a matter of cost. She carries courgettes and aubergines whenever they are cheap enough in the Dublin Corporation market. Vera sells both vegetables at the weekends and in the summer when they are in season. She carries peppers, mushrooms and garlic all the time because they sell, regardless of the cost. Her customers used to be very suspicious about peppers and suchlike but now she sells up to 20 bulbs of garlic every weekend. 'I think we're very European,' says Vera.

In the 1980s, and for long before it, Moore Street and its stalls were the natural place to go to find out just which vegetables the Irish might be suspicious of. It was considered the heart of Dublin, so quintessential as to be stereotypical of the city and its people.

In the 1990s, it began to change. An abandoned bingo hall on the street developed into an ethnic market with Chinese and African stalls. Shops opened along the street specialising in hair braiding, world music and ethnic food. A number of mobile phone shops, Asian markets and internet kiosks sprouted up. Uncertainty over future development plans for the area had meant that many of the immigrants could rent buildings at low prices, sometimes with little more than a handshake by way of a contract. They had been attracted first as customers, going for the cheap food at the market stalls, before becoming traders themselves.

Their shops became social hubs in an area of the city that, as they spread east along Parnell Street, became known as Little Africa. It has also, though, been called Chinatown. It is a *very* little Africa, and not quite a Chinatown by comparison with those in many other major cities, but in a city as small as Dublin it has had a substantial impact.

It had all changed so quickly. Diversity had become part of the cultural backdrop of the city, the country. It's easy to poke a bit of fun at a Moore Street trader's delight at selling 20 cloves of garlic as recently as 1986, and at her customers' suspicion of red peppers, when we are still in the early days of a profound change in the Irish population, its diversity, its self-identity. Any wide-eyed wonderment at the changes that have happened since will probably look equally innocent in only a few years' time.

However, Moore Street's decrepit structures are today covered in planning permission notices and posters warning the public that they enter any of the buildings at their own risk. Several of the shops have the shutters pulled down. There is energy on the street, but it is stalked by decrepitude; a sense that, while the street has been revitalised to an extent, it is only clinging on to life. A major redevelopment will demolish many of the buildings which have brought its bustle back. Hanging over Moore Street is a metaphorical wrecking ball, poised to bulldoze its newfound vitality. Although, that sounds dangerously like a prediction. And if there's anything Irish history has taught us, it's that it's best to stay away from them.

SELECT BIBLIOGRAPHY

— Abrams, L., 'The conversion of the Scandinavians of Dublin' in *Anglo-Norman Studies xx: Proceedings of the Battle Conference 1997*, Woodbridge, VA, Boydell & Brewer, 1998

— Armitage, D., *The Ideological Origins of the British Empire*, Cambridge, Cambridge University Press, 2000

— Associated Press, 'Ivan Beshoff, last survivor of the mutiny on the *Potemkin*', *New York Times*, 28 October 1987

— Ball, J. (ed.), *The Celtic Languages*, London, Routledge, 1993

— Bardon, J., *A History of Ulster*, Belfast, The Blackstaff Press, 2001

— —*A History of Ireland in 250 Episodes*, Dublin, Gill & Macmillan, 2008

— Barry, T., *A History of Settlement in Ireland*, London, Routledge, 2000

— —*The Archaeology of Medieval Ireland*, London, Routledge, 1988

— Bartlett, T. & Jeffrey, K., *A Military History of Ireland*, Cambridge, Cambridge University Press, 1997

— Benidictow, O., *The Black Death, 1346–1353: The Complete History*, Woodbridge, VA, The Boydell Press, 2004

— Benson, A., *Jewish Dublin: Portraits of Life by the Liffey*, Dublin, A & A Farmar, 2007

— Boran, E. & Gribben, C., *Enforcing Reformation in Ireland and Scotland, 1550–1700*, Aldershot, Ashgate, 2006

— Bradley, D. *et al.*, 'The scale and nature of Viking settlement in Ireland from Y-chromosome admixture analysis', *European Journal of Human Genetics*, 14 (2006)

— Bradley, R., *The Prehistory of Britain and Ireland*, Cambridge, Cambridge University Press, 2007

— Breen, C. & Forsythe, W., *Boats and Shipwrecks of Ireland*, Stroud, Tempus, 2004

— Bycock, J., *Viking Age Iceland*, London, Penguin, 2001

— Canny, N., *Making Ireland British, 1580–1650*, Oxford, Oxford University Press, 2003

— —*The Origins of Empire: British Overseas Enterprise to the Close of the Seventeenth Century*, Oxford, Oxford University Press, 2001

— Carpenter, D. A., *The Struggle for Mastery: Britain, 1066–1284*, London, Allen Lane, 2003

— Central Statistics Office, 'Census 2006: Non-Irish Nationals Living in Ireland' (June 2008)

— Chapman, M., *The Celts: The Construction of a Myth*, London, Macmillan, 1992

— Charles-Edwards, T. M., *Early Christian Ireland*, Cambridge, Cambridge University Press, 2000

— Clark, P. & Gillespie, R. (eds.), *Two Capitals: London and Dublin, 1500–1840*, Oxford, Oxford University Press for the British Academy, 2001

— Clarke, B. *et al.*, *Ireland and Scandinavia in the Early Viking Age*, Dublin, Four Courts Press, 1998

— Clarkson, L. & Crawford, E. M., *Feast and Famine: Food and Nutrition in Ireland, 1500–1920*, Oxford, Oxford University Press, 2001

— Connolly, S. J., *The Oxford Companion to Irish History*, Oxford, Oxford University Press, 2002

— Cooney, G., *Landscapes of Neolithic Ireland*, London, Routledge, 2000

— Cooney, G. & Grogan, E., *Irish Prehistory: A Social Perspective*, Dublin, Wordwell, 1994

— Coulton, G. G., *Chaucer and his England*, New York, Russell & Russell, 1957

— Cullen, P., *Refugees and Asylum-Seekers in Ireland*, Cork, Cork University Press, 2000

— Cunliffe, B., *The Ancient Celts*, Oxford, Oxford University Press, 1997

— Curl, J. S., *The Londonderry Plantation 1609–1914. The History, Architecture, and Planning of the Estates of the City of London and its Livery Companies in Ulster*, Chichester, Phillimore & Co. Ltd, 1986

— Davies, H. & Davies, M. H., *French Huguenots in English-Speaking Lands*, New York, Lang, 2000

— Devoy, Dr R., 'Sea level changes and Ireland', *Technology Ireland*, 22:5 (1990)

— Dolan, T., 'Writing in Ireland' in D. Wallace (ed.), *The Cambridge History of Medieval English Literature*, Cambridge, Cambridge University Press, 2002

— Doorley, T., 'Italy to Ireland', *Irish Times*, 21 January 2006

— Duffy, S., 'The royal dynasties of Dublin and the Isles in the eleventh century' in S. Duffy (ed.), *Medieval Dublin VII: Proceedings of the Friends of Medieval Dublin Symposium 2005*, Dublin, Four Courts Press, 2006

— Duffy, S. *et al.*, *Medieval Ireland: An Encyclopedia*, London, Routledge, 2005

— Edwards, D., 'Atrocities: some days two heads and some days four' in *History Ireland*, 17:1 (January/February 2009)

— Edwards, D. *et al.*, *Age of Atrocity: Violence and Political Conflict in Early Modern Ireland*, Dublin, Four Courts Press, 2007

— Edwards, N., *The Archaeology of Early Medieval Ireland*, London, Routledge, 1990

— Egan, P. M., 'Charles Bianconi & public transport', *www.waterfordcounty-museum.org* (January 2005)

— Eogan, G. & Herity, M., *Ireland in Prehistory*, London, Routledge, 1996

— Fahey, T. *et al.*, *Best of Times?: The Social Impact of the Celtic Tiger*, Dublin, Institute of Public Administration, 2007

— Fanning, B., *Racism and Social Change in the Republic of Ireland*, Manchester, Manchester University Press, 2002

— Fitzgerald, P. & Lambkin B., *Migration in Irish History, 1607–2007*, Basingstoke, Palgrave Macmillan, 2007

— Flanagan, L., *Ancient Ireland: Life Before the Celts*, Dublin, Gill & Macmillan, 1998

— Foster, R. F., *The Oxford History of Ireland*, Oxford, Oxford University Press, 1989

— Fraser, U. & Harvey, C. J., *Sanctuary in Ireland: Perspectives on Asylum Law and Policy*, Dublin, Institute of Public Administration, 2003

— Freeman, P., *Ireland and the Classical World*, Austin, University of Texas, 2001

— Geraghty, T. & Whitehead, T., *The Dublin Fire Brigade: A History of the Brigade, the Fires and the Emergencies*, Dublin, Four Courts Press, 2004

— Graham, B., *In Search of Ireland: A Cultural Geography*, London, Routledge, 1997

— Graham-Campbell, J. & Wilson, D., *The Viking World*, n.p., Frances Lincoln Ltd, 2001

— Gravett, C. & Nicolle, D., *The Normans: Warrior Knights and their Castles*, Oxford, Osprey Publishing, 2007

— Green, M. J., *The Celtic World*, London, Routledge, 1996

— Hadfield, A. & McVeagh, J., *Strangers to that Land: British Perceptions of Ireland from the Reformation to the Famine*, Buckinghamshire, Smyth, 1994

— Hale, A. & Payton, P., *New Directions in Celtic Studies*, Exeter, University of Exeter Press, 2000

— Hall, R., *Exploring the World of the Vikings*, London, Thames & Hudson, 2007

— Hall, R. A., 'A Viking-age grave in Donnybrook, Co. Dublin', *Medieval Archaeology*, 22 (1978)

— Halpin, A. & Newman, C., *Ireland: An Oxford Archaeological Guide to Sites from Earliest Times to AD 1600*, Oxford, Oxford University Press, 2006

— —*Handbook for Travellers in Ireland*, London, John Murray, 1866

— Hansen, M., *A Comparative Study of Thirty City-State Cultures: An Investigation*, Copenhagen, Kgl. Danske Videnskabernes Selskab, 2000

— Harbison, P., *Pre-Christian Ireland: From the First Settlers to the Early Celts*, London, Thames & Hudson, 1988

— Harper, M., *Emigrant Homecomings: The Return Movement of Emigrants, 1600–2000*, Manchester, Manchester University Press, 2005

— Harriss, G., *Shaping the Nation: England 1360–1461*, Oxford, Oxford University Press, 2007

— Healy, C., 'Carnaval do Galway: The Brazilian community in Gort, 1999–2006', *Irish Migration Studies in Latin America*, 4:3 (July 2006). Available at www.irlandeses.org

— —'"Foreigners of this kind": Chilean refugees in Ireland, 1973–1990', *Irish Migration Studies in Latin America*, 4:4 (October 2006). Available at www.irlandeses.org

— Henriksen, L., 'Viking voyage—extended interviews' for BBC's *Timewatch*, 2007, www.open2.net/timewatch/2008/vikingvoyage_extras.html

— Hobsbawm, E. & Ranger, T. (eds.), *The Invention of Tradition*, Cambridge, Cambridge University Press, 1983

— Holfter, G., *German-Speaking Exiles in Ireland 1933–1945*, Amsterdam, Rodopi, 2006

— Hutchinson, J., *The Dynamics of Cultural Nationalism: The Gaelic Revival and the Creation of the Irish Nation State*, London, Allen and Unwin, 1987

— Hylton, R., *Ireland's Huguenots and their Refuge, 1662–1745: An Unlikely Haven*, Brighton, Sussex Academic Press, 2005

— James, S., *The Atlantic Celts, Ancient People or Modern Invention?*, London, British Museum Press, 1999

— Johnson, Ruth, *Viking Age Ireland*, Dublin, TownHouse, 2004

— Johnstone, P. & McGrail, S., *The Sea-Craft of Prehistory*, London, Routledge, 1989

— Kelly, F., *A Guide to Early Irish Law*, Dublin, Dublin Institute for Advanced Studies, 1998

— Kelly, M., *A History of the Black Death in Ireland*, Stroud, Tempus, 2001

— —*The Great Dying: The Black Death in Dublin*, Stroud, Tempus, 2003

— Keogh, D., *Jews in Twentieth-Century Ireland: Refugees, Anti-Semitism and the Holocaust*, Cork, Cork University Press, 1998

— Kidd, C., *British Identities Before Nationalism: Ethnicity and Nationhood in the Atlantic World, 1600–1800*, Cambridge, Cambridge University Press, 1999

— Koch, J. T., *Celtic Culture: A Historical Encyclopaedia*, Santa Barbara, ABC-Clio, 2006

— Larsen, A., *The Vikings in Ireland*, Roskilde, The Viking Ship Museum, 2001

— Lawless Lee, G., *The Huguenot Settlements in Ireland*, Maryland, Heritage Books, 2001

— Lenihan, P., *Consolidating Conquest: Ireland 1603–1727*, London, Pearson, 2008

— Lennon, C., 'Dublin's great explosion of 1597', *History Ireland*, 3:3 (autumn 1995)

— Lennon, J., *Irish Orientalism: A Literary and Intellectual History*, Syracuse, Syracuse University Press, 2004

— Levene, M. & Roberts, P., *The Massacre in History*, New York, Berghahn Books, 1999

— Leyburn, J. G., *The Scotch-Irish: A Social History*, Chapel Hill, NC, University of North Carolina Books, 1962
— Lydon, J. F., *The Making of Ireland: From Ancient Times to the Present*, London, Routledge, 1998
— Mac Cormaic, R., 'Faraway fields give Vila Gort new gloss', *Irish Times*, 11 April 2007
— —'A new-look nation, lacking integration', *Irish Times*, 11 August 2007
— McCoy, G., 'A history of Protestant Irish speakers', www.ultach.dsl.pipex.com, 2009
— McCullough, D. W., *Wars of the Irish Kings: A Thousand Years of Struggle, from the Age of Myth through the Reign of Queen Elizabeth 1*, New York, Random House Inc., 2002
— McKie, R., *Face of Britain: How our Genes Reveal the History of Britain*, London, Simon & Schuster, 2006
— Maguire, M., *Differently Irish: A Cultural History Exploring Twenty-five Years of Vietnamese-Irish Identity*, Dublin, Woodfield Press, 2004
— Mitchell, F. & Ryan, M., *Reading the Irish Landscape*, Dublin, TownHouse, 1997
— Monk, M. & Sheehan, J., *Early Medieval Munster: Archaeology, History and Society*, Cork, Cork University Press, 1998
— Morash, C., *A History of Irish Theatre, 1601–2000*, Cambridge, Cambridge University Press, 2002
— Nyland, E., *Linguistic Archaeology: An Introduction*, Victoria, BC, Trafford Publishing, 2006
— O'Connell, C., 'Digging up a different past', *Irish Times*, 23 August 2008
— O'Connor, P., *People Make Places: The Story of the Irish Palatines*, Newcastle West, Limerick, Oireacht na Mumhan Books, 1989
— Ó Corrain, D., *Ireland Before the Normans*, Dublin, Gill & Macmillan, 1972
— Ó Cróinín, D. (ed.), *A New History of Ireland: Prehistoric and Early Ireland*, n.p., Oxford University Press, 2005
— Ó Dochartaigh, C., 'Irish in Ireland' in G. Price, *Languages in Britain and Ireland*, Oxford, Blackwell, 2000
— Ó Gráda, C., *Jewish Ireland in the Age of Joyce: A Socioeconomic History*, Princeton, NJ, Princeton University Press, 2006
— O'Kelly, M. & O'Kelly, C., *Newgrange: Archaeology, Art and Legend*, London, Thames & Hudson, 1982
— O'Neill, R. K. (ed.), *Management of Library and Archival Security: From the Outside Looking in*, New York, Haworth Press, 1998
— Ó Siochrú, M., *God's Executioner: Oliver Cromwell and the Conquest of Ireland*, London, Faber and Faber, 2008
— Otway-Ruthven, A. J., *A History of Medieval Ireland*, London, Ernest Benn Ltd, 1968

— Owens, Margaret E., *Stages of Dismemberment: The Fragmented Body in Late Medieval and Early Modern Drama*, Delaware, OH, University of Delaware Press, 2005
— Patterson, O., *Slavery and Social Death: A Comparative Study*, Cambridge, MA, Harvard University Press, 1982
— Pennell, C. R., *Bandits at Sea: A Pirates Reader*, New York, New York University Press, 2001
— Pringle, P., *Jolly Roger: The Story of the Great Age of Piracy*, New York, Courier Dover Publications, 2001
— Raftery, J., *Pagan Celtic Ireland: The Enigma of the Irish Iron Age*, London, Thames & Hudson, 1998
— Refugee Trust International, 'Reintegration policies and approaches within the EU: the case in the Republic of Ireland', May 2002, www.reintegration.net/ireland/index.htm
— Roche, R., *The Norman Invasion of Ireland*, Dublin, Anvil, 1970
— Ronan, Ambassador Sean G., 'The Palatines in Ireland: An Account of their Settlement in the 18th Century: Lecture given to the German-Irish Society at the House of the Rhineland-Palatinate Representation in Bonn, 8th February 1973', www.users.bigpond.com/olavemil/ambassador.htm
— Roth, J. P., *The Logistics of the Roman Army at War (264 BC–AD 235)*, Leiden, Brill, 1999
— Ryan, D., 'Fr John Creagh CSSR, social reformer 1870–1947', *The Old Limerick Journal*, 39 (winter 2003)
— —'Hungarians in Limerick, 1956–58', *The Old Limerick Journal*, 37 (summer 2001)
— Ryan, M., *The Illustrated Archaeology of Ireland*, Dublin, TownHouse, 1991
— Schuldes, S., 'Assimilation of the Irish Palatines During the 18th and 19th Century', Anglistiches Seminar, Heidelberg University, 24 February 2005, www.cl.uni-heidelberg.de/~schuldes/palatineTermPaper.pdf
— Seecamp, G., 'Getting a taste of the continent', *Irish Times*, 30 September 1986
— Shrewsbury, J. D. F., *A History of Bubonic Plague in the British Isles*, Cambridge, Cambridge University Press, 2005
— Sims-Williams, P., 'Celtomania and celtoscepticism', *Cambrian Medieval Celtic Studies*, 18 (1998)
— Smith, B. (ed.), *Britain and Ireland, 900–1300: Insular Responses to Medieval European Change*, Cambridge, Cambridge University Press, 1999
— Smith, C., *Late Stone Age Hunters of the British Isles*, London, Routledge, 1992
— Somerset Fry, P. & Somerset Fry, F., *A History of Ireland*, London, Routledge, 1991

— Sprague, M., *Norse Warfare: The Unconventional Battle Strategies of the Ancient Vikings*, New York, Hippocrene Books, 2007
— Stout, G., *Newgrange and the Bend of the Boyne*, Cork, Cork University Press, 2002
— Thorpe, N., 'Origins of war: mesolithic conflict in Europe', *British Archaeology*, 52 (April 2000)
— Triandafyllidou, A. & Gropas, R., *European Immigration: A Sourcebook*, Aldershot, Ashgate, 2007
— Valante, Mary A., *The Vikings in Ireland: Settlement, Trade and Urbanization*, Dublin, Four Courts Press, 2008
— Viney, E., *Ireland: A Smithsonian Natural History*, Belfast, The Blackstaff Press, 2003
— Wallace, P., *Aspects of Viking Dublin (1. Houses, 2. Clothing and Personal Ornament, 3. The Town, 4. Commerce, 5. Dublin in 988, 6. Crafts)*, Dublin, n.p., 1988
— —'Dublin's waterfront at Wood Quay: 900–1317' in G. Milne & B. Hobley (eds.), *Waterfront archaeology in Britain and northern Europe (papers of the First International Congress on Waterfront Archaeology)*, London, April 1979
— —'Viking voyage—extended interviews' for BBC's *Timewatch*, 2007, www.open2.net/timewatch/2008/vikingvoyage_extras.html
— Walton, J. K., *Fish and Chips and the British Working Class, 1870–1940*, Leicester, Leicester University Press, 1994
— Watson, A. M. & McKnight, E., 'Race and ethnicity in Northern Ireland: the Chinese community' in P. Hainsworth, *Divided Society: Ethnic Minorities and Racism in Northern Ireland*, London, Pluto Press, 1998
— White, V., 'Muslims in Little Jerusalem', *Irish Times*, 14 September 1993
— Whittle, A. W. R., *The Archaeology of People: Dimensions of Neolithic Life*, London, Routledge, 2003
— Wolf, K., *Daily Life of the Vikings*, Westport, Greenwood Publishing Group, 2004
— Wright, T. (ed.), *The historical works of Giraldus Cambrensis containing the Topography of Ireland, and the History of the Conquest of Ireland, translated by T. Forester. The Itinerary through Wales, and the Description of Wales, translated by Sir R.C. Hoare*, London, HG Bohn, 1863
— Yau, N., 'Celtic tiger, hidden dragon: exploring identity among second generation Chinese in Ireland', *Translocations* (September 2007)

INDEX